Reflections on God

Dr. Justin W. Tull

Copyright 2018

Reflections on God

Copyright 2018 © Justin W. Tull
All rights Reserved

No part of this book may be reproduced or transmitted in any form or by any means, electronic or mechanical, including photocopying and recording or by any information storage or retrieval system.
Cover and interior design by Sidewalk Labs.

Requests for permission should be addressed to
justinwtull@gmail.com

ISBN-13: 9781546848257

Scripture Quotations, unless otherwise indicated, are from New Revised Standard Version Bible, Copyright 1989 National Council of the Churches of Christ in the United States of America.
Used by permission. All rights reserved.

CONTENTS

INTRODUCTION	1
REFLECTIONS ON GOD	3
STAIRCASE OF HEAVEN	4
GOD OF ALL THE NATIONS	12
WHY GOD, WHY?	22
EVERYTHING WORKING FOR GOOD?	33
TIT FOR TAT; NOT THAT!	41
WHO IS GOD?	48
WHO IS JESUS?	56
IS CHRISTIANITY THE ONLY WAY?	65

STUDY GUIDE:

INTRODUCTION	80
STAIRCASE OF HEAVEN!	81
GOD OF ALL THE NATIONS	82
WHY GOD, WHY?	83
EVERYTHING WORKING FOR GOOD?	84
TIT FOR TAT; NOT THAT!	85
WHO IS GOD?	86
WHO IS JESUS?	87
IS CHRISTIANITY THE ONLY WAY?	88

ACKNOWLEDGEMENTS

I am deeply indebted to many persons for the content of this book. My first acknowledgement is to Dr. Albert Outler who was an early mentor and guide in my faith development. To Dr. W. J. A. Power, I am indebted for his guidance in understanding the Old Testament. In preaching, the most influential by far was Dr. Fred Craddock. To all of these I am immensely grateful for the shaping and sharpening of my theological reflection.

Many have also been a part of the technical aspects of the book. Aaron Stout has been my faithful and skilled guide for layout, design, and general feedback. Without his valuable expertise, I would not have been able to complete the five books that we have produced together.

The essential proofing of this book has been done by Margaret Jarvis, and my wife, Janette Tull. In addition, Janette has offered countless helpful suggestions that have greatly improved the book's readability.

Lastly, I am indebted to the eleven churches I have served whose nurture, feedback, example, and counsel have helped me to continue to grow as pastor and as an interpreter of the faith.

INTRODUCTION

Let me begin with an honest confession. Several months ago, my wife, Janette, finally approved the last revision of the title for my book, *Reflections on God*. She had strongly advocated for the word 'reflections' in the title. For her the word 'reflections' did not carry any negative baggage by sounding too 'religious' or too 'churchy.' However, in using my wife's preference I feel obligated to disclose that six of these so-called 'reflections' are actually 'sermons'—the precise word my wife did not want me to use in the title. In addition to the six sermons, I have added two manuscripts (*Who Is God?* and *Who Is Jesus?*) that were taken from a lectureship I did in First United Methodist Church, Crossett, Arkansas. But whether sermons or lecture, I trust that these 'reflections' are religious in the best sense of the word. They are unapologetically grounded in scripture. They are also thoroughly covered with the grit of daily life and are therefore not only relevant but less 'churchy' than one might first assume. Afterall, sermons, in their best form, are always explicitly connected to both scripture that gives direction for living, and life's struggles that often cry out for help.

How Reflections Came into Being

I can now trace the earliest contribution to this book back to the year 2001 when I was invited to preach at a non-denominational chapel in the small community of Cuchara, Colorado, where my wife and I frequent our summer cabin. (The photo on the cover of the book comes from this spectacular slice of God's creation.) From the very first sermon preached there to the many that would follow, I chose to preach only my 'favorite' sermons, those that were key to my personal faith. They also included many biblical texts that are central to my theology. In addition, these sermons encompassed many of my heart-felt convictions, my basic approach to life, and my moral values. The kernels of truth contained in these messages have also been validated by challenging circumstances, poignant experiences, and even tragic events.

The First of the 'Reflections' Series

This first book draws from sermons primarily focused on the nature of God. The two books to follow will center first on daily Christian living and then upon the essential tenets of the faith. Each of these three books will follow the same pattern: the citing of the biblical text, the manuscript of the sermon, followed by a study guide intended primarily for group use. My fervent hope is that these reflections will be a resource for faith development by deepening the reader's understanding of the Christian faith and inviting him or her to apply such insights to daily living. With such hopes let us begin.

Reflections on God

The reader should be aware that the basic assertions of this book are often in direct conflict with some prevalent theologies of our day, especially those that are an exotic blend of culture and religion. A theology grounded in Scripture promises new insights about God and life. Such biblical theology will often challenge our childhood religious thinking, our cultural prejudices, and our human tendency to create a God of our own liking.

THEOLOGY AND CULTURE

This book will often challenge theologies that have been skewed by popular culture. When some offer an image of God that strongly favors their own country, the Bible proclaims a *God of all the nations*. When some suggest that God bestows blessing with exact fairness, the Bible reveals a God who scatters blessings with reckless abandon—even providing good things for the undeserving. When one suggests that God protects *good people* from severe tragedy, both life experiences and the Scriptures call such favoritism into question. When our strong allegiance to the Christian faith seduces us into believing that God rejects the people of other faiths, the biblical message reminds us that God's claim is upon on all of God's children.

A BIBLE-CENTERED THEOLOGY

When we begin to listen more to the biblical faith and less to our dominant culture, our understanding of God can be radically transformed. Ultimately the God we discover in our honest wrestlings will prove infinitely more deserving of our deep faith and lasting obedience.

Staircase of Heaven

Genesis 28:10-17

Jacob left Beer-sheba and went towards Haran. He came to a certain place and stayed there for the night, because the sun had set. Taking one of the stones of the place, he put it under his head and lay down in that place. And he dreamed that there was a ladder set up on the earth, the top of it reaching to heaven; and the angels of God were ascending and descending on it. And the Lord stood beside him and said, 'I am the Lord, the God of Abraham your father and the God of Isaac; the land on which you lie I will give to you and to your offspring; and your offspring shall be like the dust of the earth, and you shall spread abroad to the west and to the east and to the north and to the south; and all the families of the earth shall be blessed in you and in your offspring. Know that I am with you and will keep you wherever you go and will bring you back to this land; for I will not leave you until I have done what I have promised you.' Then Jacob woke from his sleep and said, 'Surely the Lord is in this place—and I did not know it!' And he was afraid, and said, 'How awesome is this place! This is none other than the house of God, and this is the gate of heaven.'

On the way to one of our favorite spots—Cuchara, Colorado—there are many beautiful rock formations and natural wonders. One prominent landmark has been named 'The Giant Staircase.' It is a huge mass of stone that forms three gigantic steps jutting hundreds of feet from the highway below. As I think about this text, I am tempted to rename those steps the 'Staircase of Heaven.' Perhaps by the end of my reflection you will understand why.

Jacob's Ladder

As I studied this passage of scripture, I learned that I have long carried a misconception about what many have called 'Jacob's ladder.' My first surprising discovery from reading several commentaries was that they all agreed that Jacob's vision was not a ladder as we know it today, but more like a 'ramp' or 'stair-like pavement.'[1] This 'ramp' was to handle traffic between heaven and earth.[2] Heavenly messengers could thus approach those dwelling below.

After reading about Jacob's 'ladder' being a ramp-like structure, I decided to revisit the familiar song I loved to sing at summer youth camp, "We Are Climbing Jacob's Ladder." As campers, we would sing "We are climbing, higher, higher," as we made our way to the outdoor chapel. But as I began to study the song's lyrics and reflect on the biblical story, I soon discovered it was not an accurate rendering of Jacob's experience. The song simply borrowed the biblical image of 'ladder' to make a point of its own. Rather than using the imagery to speak of God or angels approaching us, the song spoke of our journey to meet God. But the Jacob story is not about Jacob or any human climbing 'higher, higher.' It is not about our efforts to move closer and closer to God. Jacob's story is about God's coming lower and lower, closer and closer, that he might be near and dear to us, his creatures. Jacob's story is not about a holy man going to a holy place to meet God. It is about a fugitive, scared of his brother's wrath, who is encountered by the God of his fathers, the God of Abraham and Isaac.

Do you know what happened prior to Jacob's dream? Jacob tricked his father into giving the family blessing to him rather than to his brother, Esau. Once his trickery was discovered, Jacob decides it is much healthier to find a new residence—and pronto! In other words, the hairy-chested brother, the great hunter, has discovered that Jacob has betrayed him, and Esau is now ready to eliminate his sibling rival forever.

RESTLESS NIGHT

So, when Jacob lies down to take his rest, it is not after attending vespers and saying his prayers—except maybe a prayer for protection. Jacob is nothing more than a fugitive on the run, stopping to get some sleep, but what he receives will be far more refreshing, far more empowering, far more advantageous than restful slumber. He receives an encounter with God: a vision of a ladder or ramp and a speech from God that renews God's promise to Abraham's descendants.

RAMPS AND ESCALATORS

I must confess that the image of this biblical story is a bit uncomfortable to me. I suppose the problem is that the 'ramp' idea reminds me too much of modern-day escalators. The image recalls my life-long frustration with those mechanical stairs in airports and malls. Let me explain my slight phobia. No matter how carefully I plan my route in a local mall, I invariably choose the wrong way. If I plan to go 'up' I might walk past cosmetics and the men's department and finally arrive at the escalator entrance, only to discover that I am standing in the front of the 'down' escalator. The 'up' escalator is inconveniently located on the opposite side of the store! Ugh!

This has happened to me so many times that I have become somewhat suspicious that escalators are engineered so that they can be rotated half a turn at will and that someone who hates either ministers or directionally challenged people like me, stands poised at the controls. If I start out in the right direction toward the right escalator, the attendant waits patiently until I am almost there and then rotates the escalator a half a turn away from me. But if I start out in the wrong direction, he allows me the privilege of messing up all by myself. It seems that whenever I arrive at the escalator, it is always going in the wrong direction. Or, to put it in existential terms, it is hard for me to find a way up when I am feeling down. It is hard to find an access to heaven when the world has dropped me into the pit.

HEAVEN AND EARTH

But our story of Jacob would have a different scenario for my dilemma. The storyline would suggest that heaven and earth are conveniently and directly connected. Even better, the biblical narrative would insist that the God on high is willing and able to come down to us, even when we least expect him, in places both holy and secular, at times when we are saints and more often when we are sinners, those times when we are feeling the 'blues' and the 'blahs.'

The story of Jacob's encounter is not about Jacob seeking God, climbing higher and higher. It is about the Creator of heaven and earth stooping lower and lower to find a fearful fugitive and then giving him a large dose of grace, an ample portion of promise, and a reassurance of his abiding presence.

When God comes down to speak with Jacob, it is not through a burning bush as with Moses. As Jacob sleeps restlessly, God reassures Jacob of his comforting presence. Jacob learns that even far from his homeland, he is not alone. Even with his sinfulness, God still approaches him. Now Jacob knows that heaven and earth can and do touch in unexpected times and places. Evidently, the God on high is not content to keep his heavenly distance.

God's Promise

In his encounter with God, Jacob also hears again the promise first made to Abraham, a promise of land and of many descendants. But in this encounter with God the main focus seems to be best captured in the image of the 'ladder' or 'ramp,' or what Jacob calls in the end of the story the 'gate of heaven. What follows is a message of hope and comfort to Jacob: "Know that I am with you and will keep you wherever you go… Behold, I am with you and will keep you wherever you go…" (Genesis 28:15)

As Jacob awaited the confrontation with his brother, he might have well expected a nightmare, but what he received was a reassuring dream. Wouldn't we like to have the gift of such a dream in the dark nights of our soul? This promise of God's presence would be a good dream any time, but especially in times of anxiety and fear. Jacob, filled with anxiety over facing his brother, would be met by the Prince of Peace who would calm his fears. Jacob now knew that God would be with him. He would not be alone.

New Christian Symbol?

Perhaps today we could use a new Christian symbol, one inherited from the Old Testament. We might choose the symbol of an ancient dirt-paved ramp, or a giant staircase, or perhaps even a modern escalator. All are intended for *dual directions*—not just up or just down but one that would incorporate both upward and downward traffic. The 'upward way' for us would also be the 'downward way' for God.

Staircase of Heaven

I do have a favorite image of the passageway between heaven and earth. My personal preference is the image of a 'staircase of heaven.' And I discover a wonderful reminder of that symbol every time I drive from LaVeta to Cuchara, Colorado—three huge steps amid green landscapes with majestic mountains in the distance. Surrounded by such beauty, I am reminded of the greatness of the Creator, but also of something more. I am reminded that this Creator God is not content to keep his distance. God comes to me as if descending these huge steps of divine creation to meet me wherever I am—in joy or in sorrow, in fear or in calm. His message to me is the same as it was to Jacob: "I will be with you."

This 'staircase of heaven' can certainly accommodate traffic in both directions. We can go up; God can come down. We can seek our Father; the Great Shepherd can and does seek us. We can climb higher. God can come lower. But we, by ourselves, can never scale the heights all the way to heaven. Earth cannot reach heaven without heaven first coming to earth.

Jacob now understands how one arrives at the 'gate of heaven.' It is not primarily by our seeking God but by God seeking us. Do you remember what Jacob said about his discovery? "Surely the Lord was in this place and I did not know it." Sound familiar? Have you ever suddenly realized that God had been with you long before you knew he was there? Have you ever been in exile or in fear only to discover that the Spirit of God had already come to your aid?

THE GOOD NEWS

The good news of Jacob's story is not simply that there are some pathways to God. The good news is not that *sometimes* God comes to us. The good news is not that heaven and earth are somehow connected, making encounters possible. The good news is revealed in Jacob's humble revelation: "Surely the Lord is in this place—and I did not know it." (Genesis 28:16)

The promise God made to Jacob was not just what *would* be or *could* be but what *is*—God is with us! God is with us in our exile and in our pain, in our apathy and confusion, in our sin and in our service, in our homeland and in every new frontier. The good news is this: God is *always* with us—whether we realize it or not.

Staircase of Heaven

I think there is a better name for the Jacob story than Jacob's 'ladder.' I like 'staircase of heaven' and I have a familiar landmark as my reminder. Notice it is not 'staircase *to* heaven' as if we could simply make our way to God on our own. It is God on high who brings the touch of heaven to us. The steps originate not on earth but in heaven. It is God who promises to be with us. It is God who connects forever heaven and earth.

I like the image of those three gigantic steps. They reflect how life really is. We seek God and God seeks us. We seek God when we are feeling religious or desperate. God seeks us even when we aren't religious. He seeks us when we are at our worse, when we don't really deserve God's presence or care. That is one reason I especially like the image of those gigantic steps—daunting for us but so well-suited for God, implying that God seeks us far more than we seek God. After all, God seeks us even when we are not looking for him.

Yet we may still seek God, and we certainly should. We should pray and worship and serve and give thanks. We should be mindful of God's presence and guidance. But we must never forget that the God we seek is already seeking us. God, in fact, will meet us in the strangest of places—not just in the sacred space of religion, but in the most mundane and earthly places imaginable. He will meet us at the tomb, at the cross, at the graveside of our grief. He will meet us in our dreams and in our hopes, in our waking and in our sleeping. He will come to us even when we are totally unaware of his presence.

THE ONE WHO COMES TO US

The One who comes to us invites us to rise and walk, to live anew, to take on earthly responsibilities. The One who meets us promises to go with us and to be with us always.

And on the good days when we find ourselves on that 'staircase' climbing 'higher and higher' hoping to get a glimpse of God, to be close to the Divine, we should not be surprised to discover that the God of Jacob is already with us!

Based on a sermon of the same title from *Wrestlings, Wonders, and Wanderers* by Justin Tull.

God of All the Nations

Genesis 12:1-3

Now the LORD said to Abram, "Go from your country and your kindred and your father's house to the land that I will show you. I will make of you a great nation, and I will bless you, and make your name great, so that you will be a blessing. I will bless those who bless you, and the one who curses you I will curse; and in you all the families of the earth shall be blessed."

Acts 10:25-34

On Peter's arrival Cornelius met him, and falling at his feet, worshipped him. But Peter made him get up, saying, "Stand up; I am only a mortal." And as he talked with him, he went in and found that many had assembled; and he said to them, "You yourselves know that it is unlawful for a Jew to associate with or to visit a Gentile; but God has shown me that I should not call anyone profane or unclean. So, when I was sent for, I came without objection. Now may I ask why you sent for me?"

Cornelius replied, "Four days ago at this very hour, at three o'clock, I was praying in my house when suddenly a man in dazzling clothes stood before me. He said, 'Cornelius, your prayer has been heard and your alms have been remembered before God. Send therefore to Joppa and ask for Simon, who is called Peter; he is staying in the home of Simon, a tanner, by the sea.' Therefore, I sent for you immediately, and you have been kind enough to come. So now all of us are here in the presence of God to listen to all that the Lord has commanded you to say."

Then Peter began to speak to them: "I truly understand that God shows no partiality, but in every nation anyone who fears him and does what is right is acceptable to him." (Acts 10:34-35)

It was in Dr. Power's class on the Old Testament that I heard for the first time what he believed to be one of the key passages of the Old Testament, one he proposed was nothing less than *the* purpose for God's chosen ones, the Hebrews. The key passage begins in this way:

> Now the Lord said to Abram, 'Go from your country and your kindred and your father's house to the land I will show you. I will make of you a great nation, and I will bless you, and make your name great... (Genesis 12:1-2)

Who does not want to hear words like these? We all want to become great. We all want to be blessed do we not? So why wouldn't the Hebrews want to be the 'chosen ones,' the 'blessed ones' of God? And why wouldn't they expect preferential treatment perhaps even God's indulgence?

A Case of Indulgence

Liz, my wife's daughter-in-law, is currently an executive for an international company and travels often overseas, leaving little opportunity some weeks for quality time with her two children. But she works diligently to carve out time when she can. Recently she returned from a week-long trip at a time when her husband and daughter had left for an overnight Indian Princess retreat. She decided to take advantage of the time with some one-on-one time with her seven-year-old son, Hudson. The next 24 hours were crammed with favorite places, tasty treats, and fun activities. Liz made their time together as special as she could.

Upon the return of father and daughter, Hudson pulled his father aside and made him a very generous offer: "Papa, if there is anything you want from Mom, just ask me and I'll get it for you!"

THE PURPOSE BEHIND BEING BLESSED

Well, if the Hebrews believed that being 'chosen' or 'blessed' would mean constant pampering, abundant material blessings and the absence of hardship, they would soon be very disappointed. Being blessed, in fact, was not about being 'indulged' at all. In fact, being 'chosen' was perhaps more a responsibility than an outright privilege. Listen to the rest of the passage that Dr. Power thought was so crucial to the Hebrews' understanding of their calling:

> I will make of you a great nation, and I will bless you, and make your name great, so that you will be a blessing. I will bless those who bless you, and the ones who curse you I will curse, and in you all the families of the earth shall be blessed.

Did you hear the purpose for the Jewish people?

> I will bless you, and make your name great, so that you will be a blessing...*in you all the families of the earth will be blessed.*

Dr. Power insisted that the purpose for the Hebrews was never to bask in their blessedness. God had not blessed them as a form of indulgence as if comfort and privilege were the proper reward for their good behavior. Instead the Hebrews were to be blessed by God *in order* that God could bless all people. Ultimately, God's blessings were not simply directed *to* them but also *through* them to others.

THE PLIGHT OF THE HEBREWS

As one observes the history of the Hebrews, it is obvious that their life story was not 'better' or 'easier' than peoples around them. Indeed, the Hebrews would be enslaved and then escape only to wander in the wilderness for decades. Later they would become a nation, only to be conquered and then exiled. Throughout many centuries the Jewish people would undergo harsh prejudice, persecution, hardship, and even genocide. Throughout this difficult journey the Hebrews remained a blessed people, still entrusted by God to bring a blessing to others.

This theology of 'universal blessing' was totally different than the predominant understanding of its day. Other prevalent theologies insisted that their God was not the God of other tribes but one devoted solely to their tribe and their self-interest. In contrast, the theology inherited by the Hebrews dared suggest that God's providence and blessing were never intended exclusively for one tribe, but always open to all people.

THE INCLUSIVE CREATION STORY

The creation story, recorded earlier in Genesis, would also have a similar theme. The Creator God of the Hebrews was not simply *their* God but the God of the whole of creation. God would not create one tribe but *all* people. In fact, all things, material and living, could be traced back to one Creator God.

Nor would this God later become primarily concerned for only his 'chosen ones.' The divine plan would remain inclusive, never exclusive. Even the promised messiah would have concern for more than just the Hebrew people. In Isaiah 49:5-6 we discover the repeated notion of inclusion:

> And now the Lord says, who formed me in the womb to be his servant, to bring Jacob back to him, and that Israel might be gathered to him, for I am honored in the sight of the Lord, and my God has become my strength—he says. "It is too light a thing that you should be my servant to raise up the tribes of Jacob and to restore the survivors of Israel; I will give you as a light to the nations, that my salvation may reach to the end of the earth."

Today we should be grateful that the Hebrew Scriptures introduced us to one of the most important aspects of God's nature and God's relationship to creation: The God we worship is the God of *all people*, the God of *every nation*.

THE NEW TESTAMENT ANSWERS

Christians should not be surprised to see Old Testament themes carry over into the New Testament. Even with the presence of intense racial, tribal and religious prejudice, the early Christian church did not revert into tribalism or to a theology of exclusion. Christianity was charged by Christ to take the gospel into the whole world, and that precluded isolationism or a theology of favoritism.

In the book of Acts, we discover that Peter has been summoned by God to speak to Cornelius, one who stood outside of Peter's faith, culture and comfort zone. Peter brought words of God's favor, words that included Peter's blessing. Listen to the gracious words of affirmation that Peter bestows on this foreigner:

> "I truly understand that God shows no partiality, but in every nation anyone who fears him and does what is right is acceptable to him." (Acts 10:34-35)

These words, spoken to Cornelius on behalf of God, are they not also intended to be our words? Are we not compelled as Christians to affirm that the God of Christians is truly the God of all peoples, the God of all creation, and the God of all nations? Should we not believe that every person who believes in God and does what is right is acceptable to God? Indeed, what would be our basis for excluding the foreigner from God's family?

God of All Nations

I find no trouble at all in believing that God is the God of all nations. The biblical message, though it affirms such a God, does not have to convince me of such truth. My own experience has already led me to that same conclusion. But then I have the real advantage of knowing personally people like Rudiger and Erika Hoffman of Germany and Oksana Petrova of St. Petersburg, Russia. I also know people of other religions and nationalities whom I believe God finds acceptable. I am not at all tempted to revert to tribalism or exclusivism, believing that my God is only the God of those who believe like me, look like me, or live in the same country. I already believe in a God of all the nations. Scripture simply affirms that the God I worship cannot be reduced to a God who serves only one tribe, one race, or one nation.

God Bless America

But some Americans still wonder, "Does God love other countries as much as he does America?" And what exactly do we mean when we say, "God bless America"? Does it mean we want God to bless us more than God blesses other countries? And what are those blessings anyway—increased standard of living, better life-style, more freedoms? If so, should Americans get more of these blessings over other countries that have almost none of these advantages?

And what would be God's intention if God were to continue to 'bless America'? Should we interpret it as a reward for our good behavior? Should we ask God to indulge us? Or would blessing America have a few strings attached, something God expects of us in return?

A Reason to Be Blessed

I am wondering if the lesson Dr. Power shared with the class decades ago might hold the key. He said that God had a purpose in blessing the Hebrews. That purpose was to bless all the peoples of the earth.

What if that same purpose was the reason for blessing America? How would blessing America bring blessing to others? Would being blessed by God suggest to us privilege or entitlement, or would it ignite an urgent sense of responsibility?

Jesus' Example

It is undeniable that Jesus brought blessing to many people. Some he healed, some he fed, some he challenged, some he transformed, and all without regard to tribe or nation. Even so, there was one group that he sought to bless more than others. Was it the religious, those deserving of his affection? Was it those in power who could help magnify Jesus's outreach?

In Luke 4:16-21 we discover the real focus of Jesus' ministry, the ones he sought most to bless.

> When he came to Nazareth, where he had been brought up, he went to the synagogue on the sabbath day, as was his custom. He stood up to read, and the scroll of the prophet Isaiah was given to him. He unrolled the scroll and found the place where it is written:
> 'The Spirit of the Lord is upon me,
>   because he has anointed me
>   to bring good news to the poor.
> He has sent me to proclaim release to the captives
>   and recovery of sight to the blind,

> to let the oppressed go free,
> to proclaim the year of the Lord's favor.'

THE ONES JESUS CHOSE

Jesus defined at the very beginning of his ministry what kind of Messiah he would be. He chose to reach out to the captives, the oppressed, the poor. Jesus would choose to make the most vulnerable the frequent recipients of his blessing.

Later near the end of his life, Jesus would make it equally clear that his followers should do the same, making the marginalized a priority for compassion and care. In the gospel of Matthew, Jesus shares his high praise for those who chose to bless those who were most needy:

> For I was hungry, and you gave me food, I was thirsty, and you gave me something to drink, I was a stranger and you welcomed me, I was naked and you gave me clothing, I was sick and you took care of me, I was in prison and you visited me. (Matthew 25:35-36)

If we are to be blessed as Americans and as Christians, we have no less responsibility than the early Hebrews. We are to take our blessing and pass it on. We have been blessed with a purpose and a responsibility, that through us the whole world and its people might be blessed.

GOD BLESS AMERICA

I sometimes wonder if we Americans make the mistake of thinking that God has blessed America because we deserve it, or because we are somehow better. Do we think we are better than the people of other countries? Wait. We *are* the people of other countries. And as a people from many lands we have some soul-searching to do. As both Christians and Americans, we might ask ourselves a few basic questions.

If we were 'God for a Day' and we could bless any country in the world with improved living conditions, greater freedoms, and more opportunities, which county would we pick? What it the only two choices were Haiti and the USA?

If our choice was to bless America, how would we choose to bless it? Material wealth? Improved standard of living? A familiar patriotic song offers a much different answer:

> God bless America, land that I love. Stand beside her and guide her, through the night with a light from above. [3]

The song's hope is simple and devoid of indulgence. God could bless America not with more material blessings, not with a higher standard of living and more 'stuff,' but with something much more valuable—the light of God's guidance and presence. And if that is not enough, the song offers another hope: "and crown thy good with brotherhood from sea to shining sea." [4]

So how indeed will God bless America and all the nations? Does God intend to bless those who are most needy? Is God counting on us to help? Are we, like the Hebrews, blessed in order that we be a blessing to others? Are we, like Jesus, called to care about the poor, the vulnerable, the sick? Are we, like Peter, asked to be open to those outside our nation, our religious preference, our race? When we say, "God Bless America," what do we mean? What are we asking God to do?

As I think about my faith and this great country I live in, I know clearly what I believe.

MY CREDO

- ❖ I believe God calls us to care more about justice than prosperity, more about compassion than free enterprise, more about world peace than national self-interest.

- ❖ I believe God asks us to shape our culture in the light of our religion, not to shape our religion to the mindset of our culture.

- ❖ I believe that as Christians, we do not worship the God of America, that our God can never be confined to one tribe, one nation, or one race.

- ❖ I believe we worship the God of all the Nations. We share the same divine spark. We belong to the same family. We are all brothers and sisters.

- ❖ I believe our God judges us not by where we are born, or the color of our skin, but by where we stand and the color of our hearts.

- ❖ I believe God calls us to be citizens of God's kingdom first, and citizens of our country second, that God calls us to help make our country and our world peaceful, loving, and just.

- ❖ I believe God invites us to be God's patriots, true citizens of the Kingdom.

Yes, the God of all creation has truly blessed America. So now may we bless others, ourselves and the whole world around us.

Why God, Why?

2 Corinthians 1: 3-4

Blessed be the God and Father of our Lord Jesus Christ, the Father of mercies and the God of all comfort, who comforts us in all our affliction, so that we may be able to comfort those who are in any affliction, with the comfort with which we ourselves are comforted by God. (RSV)

Have you ever asked the question: "Why God, why?" Have you ever asked why God allows the death of innocent children? Have you ever asked why God does not prevent life-threatening illnesses? Have you ever asked why God gives people the freedom to bring terrible harm to so many people?

How could the Creator of everything permit so many terrible tragedies to scourge his beloved creation? Is God indifferent to our plight? Does God remain detached to the suffering so present in our current world?

Encounter with Tragedy

In my many years of ministry I have certainly witnessed countless tragedies. I have tried to offer consolation to many who were overwhelmed by a sense of loss or betrayal or injustice.

One of the most heart-wrenching experiences was ministering to a man who lost his wife. They had only been in the Dallas area for a few months. His wife had been under psychiatric care before they moved. But the psychiatrist thought she was stable enough to make the move. She had visited our church only a few times before I received word that she had died. When I went to visit with her husband, I learned the depth of the tragedy. She had taken her own life. Equally tragic was that her unborn child died with her. Her husband could do little but sob incessantly. I was deeply touched by his immense grief.

My life in ministry has been filled with such tragic circumstances, covering the wide spectrum of circumstances.

- I have officiated a service of a still-born child.
- I consoled a family whose runaway child had lost both legs as he tried to jump on a moving train.
- I have stood with a sister as we watched her brother die at only seventeen years of age, a victim of leukemia.

In each of these tragedies I was shaken to the core. My heart went out to those who were so overwhelmed by loss and grief. The enormity of the tragedy did not escape me.

POSSIBILITY OF COMFORT AND NEW LIFE

But I also insist that none of these experiences was devoid of love or hope. As I stood by those facing life's dark valleys, I have witnessed compassion in those poignant moments. I felt a special closeness to those who were suffering. Because of my faith, I continued to believe that life was not over for them. Even as dark as the moment was, I believed the future had some promise of life and light.

- As I performed the service for the woman who took her own life and that of her unborn child, I was touched that five executives from Dow Jones flew from New York to Dallas to sit with the distraught husband during the memorial service. He was not alone in his hour of deep suffering.
- I watched the young boy who had lost both legs racing down the hospital hallway on a skateboard, grinning from ear to ear.
- Years after burying a still-born child, I would baptize an infant born to that same young couple.

- As I watched a young seventeen-year old boy draw his last breath, I sensed the cruelty of his premature death. But I also felt a peace that filled the room. I think that peace was a sign that he had entered a new realm, a realm unlike his battle with cancer, a realm devoid of pain and tears. At his passing, his older sister embraced me tightly as grief overwhelmed her. I felt an unexpected closeness to one I hardly knew. We had been united in our humanness.

All of us have experienced tragic moments, some striking closer to home than others. We have all felt the sting of such losses. Some of us will face such times with hope. Others will experience despair or anger. Some will even challenge God's justice and cry out: "Why God, why? Why do you allow natural disasters, terminal illness, acts of terrorism? Do you not care?"

WILLIAM SLOAN COFFIN: A FELLOW SUFFERER

In more recent years the theology of William Sloan Coffin (1924-2006) has become a welcome mantra for my own theology of suffering. Coffin was a nationally known Presbyterian minister who served as pastor of Riverside Church in New York City. In 1983, his 24-year-old son, Alex, was killed when his car accidently crashed into the Boston harbor during a rainstorm.

Ten days following the death of his son, Reverend Coffin stepped into the pulpit to share both his intense sorrow for a beloved son and his firm conviction in a compassionate God. In his message, Coffin confessed that he did not appreciate some of the empty and erroneous words spoken to him by people hoping to ease his pain. Those who insisted that his son's death was somehow God's will especially fueled his anger and triggered this personal reflection:

> For some reason, nothing so infuriates me as the incapacity of seemingly intelligent people to get it through their heads that God doesn't go around this world with his fingers on triggers, his fists around knives, his hands-on steering wheels. God is dead set against all unnatural deaths. [5]

For Coffin, God was first a God of comfort: "My own consolation lies in knowing that it was not the will of God that Alex die; that when the waves closed over the sinking car, God's heart was the first of all our hearts to break." [6]

A NEW MANTRA

Coffin, as he wrestled with the painful loss of his own son, was able to proclaim to his gathered congregation his belief in God's role during those tumultuous days. He told them, "God provides *minimum protection, and maximum support.*"

MINIMUM PROTECTION

In recent years, I have found the mantra of *minimum protection, maximum support* to be a clear and concise description of my theology of tragedy. True, it falls short of what many of us want to believe and experience. We want to believe instead in a God of *maximum* protection. But such a position is not supported by either the biblical witness or life experience. Biblical characters rarely enjoy an abundance of 'protection' from the suffering and hardships of life. Quite the contrary, many of them receive an abundance of hard times, even more severe than many of their contemporaries.

Experiences in life also support the notion of *minimum protection*. As a minister, I have witnessed countless tragedies experienced by 'good people,' those who from my perspective did not deserve such suffering. These frequent tragic occurrences certainly support the notion that faithful people receive only minimum protection by God. Or to put it another way, people of faith, people of strong character and moral discernment, seem to receive no *special* protection from God as if they must be rewarded for their good behavior. For me, both the biblical faith and the experiences of life, support the notion that God does not 'play favorites' by offering protection and favor to those who faithfully serve him. As much as we might want special treatment and to be freed from a sense of vulnerability, I believe we are left with only 'minimum protection.' However, many within the religious community continue to question such a stance. They insist that God not only rewards faithfulness with prosperity, but also provides a safeguard to many of the tragedies and hardships of life.

Maximum Support

The second half of Coffin's mantra garners a strong consensus from the religious community. Few Christians would argue against a God of *maximum support*. Both the biblical faith and Christian dogma insist that God is always a God of maximum support. Yet during tragedy and crisis, people of faith may not always feel such support from God. Some may cry out that God has abandoned them at a time of greatest need. In the face of such doubt, the community of faith quietly insists that God does indeed offer support, for such has been both their inner conviction and their personal experience. They continue to believe that God is 'always with us' and especially in times of tragedy—even in the 'valley and shadow of death.' They continue to believe in a God of *maximum support*.

For most of my ministry, I have believed in a theology of suffering consistent with Coffin's mantra of 'minimum protection and maximum support.' But it was only through the crucible of a personal encounter with tragedy that I would claim it with even greater certainty. I would come to know through my own experience that my God, though not protecting me from tragedy, was ever with me, offering not only comfort, but ultimately the power to find meaning and joy amid a life-and- death struggle.

Tragedy Strikes Close at Home

I remember so clearly that call at eight in the morning following my wife's MRI the night before. The neurosurgeon words seemed so void of emotion: "If possible, I need to see you and your wife in my office in thirty minutes to discuss Mrs. Tull's MRI." After a ten-minute drive to Presbyterian hospital we were soon staring up at an image of my wife's brain. There was a clearly discernable mass even to our untrained eyes. The surgeon tried to explain what this all meant. "It is a glioblastoma multiforme brain tumor, located near the brain stem. We don't know the stage yet but I'm afraid it will be a grade three or grade four, the fastest growing kind. In a few days I can surgically remove it, but it will grow back." "Where's the hope in that?" my wife asked. "I don't know," was the surgeon's only response.

My wife and I walked to the car in silence, totally shell-shocked from the events of that morning. Then my wife, Lynn, proved she had already processed her situation. "I have two choices," she said. "I can have a pity party or go on with my life." I was quite sure she had already made her choice. It was a choice from which she would never waver, not even once during her 27-month battle with cancer. My wife was going to "get on with her life!"

Never once during her illness did Lynn ever complain to me of the unfairness of her ordeal. She shed very few tears in my presence. The only time I remember her crying for any length of time was after she attempted to read to Owen, her small grandson. The weakness to her left side, a result of the tumor's growth, made it very difficult for her to hold both him and the book as she read. When she finally finished her grandmother duties and was left alone in her chair she began to quietly sob. "I can't be the kind of grandmother I had hoped to be." In my memory, this was one of her few outward expressions of regret, though I am sure she had many.

Once near the end of her life, I decided to share some of my feelings about losing her. We were lying side by side in the bed neither quite ready to get up and prepare for the day. "I'm really going to miss you," I said without daring to look at her. "Where are you going?" she said, obviously oblivious to the real meaning of my words. She was far too intent on living, to be focused on dying.

THE AUTHOR'S WRESTLINGS

Lynn had her attitude toward her illness and I had mine. Both of us were focused on making the most of our time together. Neither of us spent time bewailing our lot. What good would that do? A close friend of the family even asked me if Lynn's illness had shaken my faith. My answer? "Absolutely not! It has shaken me to the core, but not my faith."

My experience in life, enriched by being with families who suffered many, many tragedies, had helped my theology of suffering to mature. Indeed, I had been responsible for interpreting the tragedies of life through the lens of faith, not only through funeral messages but through my gift of reassuring hope as I offered a quiet presence to those grieving and fearful and overwhelmed.

I don't believe I had yet discovered Coffin's statement of faith, but I believed its affirmation completely. I shared Coffin's view that the God I worshipped is a God of *minimum protection*, and *maximum support*. I had believed such for decades, I am sure, but now it was being tested in a most severe way. My wife of fifty-six years of age was dying of cancer, and I could do nothing to stop it. But I did have a choice. I could choose how I would deal with it, how I would be husband and father and minister during that challenging, but also meaningful and intimate time.

SUFFICIENT GRACE

I also had more than Coffin's poignant phrase to guide and comfort me. I had a biblical mantra that became a faith heartbeat during my wife's illness and subsequent death. It came from an account of Paul, described in his letter to the church at Corinth. In the account, found in 2 Corinthians 12:7-10, Paul shares with his readers that he has an aggravating condition, one he describes as a "thorn in the flesh." He never discloses the nature of this 'thorn,' whether physical or mental, but one easily assumes it was a major burden for him. Three times he prays to God for God to remove this nagging condition, but the 'thorn' was not removed. What God gave instead of 'a change of circumstance' was to give Paul reassurance that he would be able to deal with it. You might say that Paul experienced 'minimum protection' and no special treatment. What would God give in its place?

What God gave was simply words, words of encouragement. God responded to Paul's pleas for help with this message of hope: *"My grace is sufficient for you, for my power is made perfect in weakness."*

During those 27 months of Lynn's illness, God's grace was also sufficient for me, empowering me to be a loving caregiver for my wife. I never assumed I was stumbling through those days equipped only with my own inner strength. My own inner goodness was not enough for the hour. Only by God's grace was I able to be husband and father and minister during such difficult days.

God of Comfort

My experience with personal tragedy also reminded me of another passage of scripture, that of our biblical text. By this time in my life, I had committed its comforting words to memory. But now the words would be more than *in* my mind and *on* my tongue; they would be as a *heartbeat* along my treacherous journey. I would experience daily a 'God of comfort.'

But my text promised the possibility of even more. Paul rightly insists that God intends not only to bestow comfort to his children himself, but also to empower us to do the same. The text concludes with the words: "so that you may be able to comfort those who are in any affliction with the comfort with which you are comforted by God." These words are indeed "grace-filled." Sometimes the comfort we receive from others will be equally conducive to our healing.

I must insist that during those trying times this passage of scripture was fully realized. By that I mean that during difficulty and impending grief, I received not only God's grace, but also the renewing gifts of friends, family, and church. Perhaps God's grace alone might have been enough, but I am infinitely grateful that the love and support of others was amply present as well.

Tragedy: No Surprise for a Christian

As Christians, we should not be disillusioned when tragedy comes our way. After all, our symbol of hope is the cross, and the cross was first an instrument of death, a horrible and painful death. If we are good students of the Bible and of life, we know that we are all vulnerable. No one will be exempt from tragedy and pain. After all, we worship a

God who did not prevent the greatest injustice of all, the crucifixion of his only Son. Nor did the Son save himself.

Even Jesus received *minimum protection.* Jesus, like us, was vulnerable. Jesus, like us, suffered injustice and pain and tragedy.

But, ah, then came Easter. Love was not defeated—not for Jesus, not for God's children, not for us! There would be life after the cross, joy after sorrow, laughter after tears. Our faith proclaims that there is the possibility of victory and new life in the face of every tragedy. Even when death comes prematurely, even when terrorism rears its ugly head, even when the misuse of human freedom costs the lives of hundreds of people, God offers comfort, support and strength.

BAD NEWS/ GOOD NEWS

Make no mistake; there is still bad news. The bad news is this: "We are vulnerable!" We can suffer tragedy, illness, injustice, even death. We can lose those we dearly love. But the 'Good News' is that God is *with* us. The 'Good News' is that we can have the privilege of being there for others, of giving comfort in the same manner that God has comforted us.

In the face of human tragedy, I am thoroughly convinced that God is a God of 'minimum protection and maximum support.' And that is enough for me. And yet there is more. The comfort God brings is invariably followed by the comfort of others. And more. The comfort we receive, we can pass on to others who suffer. We can comfort as we have been comforted. Paul was absolutely right about the loving nature of God and the sacred privilege of being able to share both our pain and our comfort.

> Blessed be the God and Father of our Lord Jesus
> Christ, the Father of mercies and the God of all

comfort, who comforts us in all our affliction, so that we may be able to comfort those who are in any affliction, with the comfort with which we ourselves are comforted by God. (2 Cor. 1:3-4)

Based on a sermon of the same title from *Why God, Why? Sermons on the Problem of Pain* by Justin Tull

Everything Working for Good?

Romans 8:28

> We know that in everything God works for good with those who love him, who are called according to his purpose. (RSV)

In Romans 8:28 Paul makes perhaps the most daring claim of his ministry! It is a claim he makes not only for himself, but also for the Christians in Rome. Some would argue he even speaks for us when he says, "We know that in everything God works for good with those who love him, who are called according to his purpose."

PAUL'S OUTLANDISH CLAIM

But do we believe that "in everything God works for good"? Are we willing to join in Paul's outlandish claim? Are we willing to defend this position to those who stand outside the faith? Can we suggest to others our conviction that no matter how bad things seem right now, God will work to see that things work out for good? Is this just wishful thinking or is it really true?

Can we hold fast in believing in God's ability to resurrect good out of tragedy, injustice, evil acts, failure, natural disaster, betrayal, child abuse, sickness and even death? Is God able to bring good out of these terrible circumstances? Paul is not suggesting that God *causes* all things to happen. He is not suggesting that God *wills* these happenings *in order to bring about good*. Paul is not even suggesting that *all things work out for the best*.

Paul's claim is that even when things are not as they

should be, when events occur that are counter to God's will, when life is undeniably tragic, God is able in and through these experiences to bring about good, a good that even we can discern.

If Paul is right, then some will need to rethink their understanding of God. Rather than thinking that God's role is to prevent tragedy, we can envision a God always present in the midst of tragedy, bringing about healing and even blessing. God does not send these crises to test us or help us to grow. God does not ignite the fires that threaten to destroy us. Rather, God helps us fight the flames. And when great tragedy comes, God stoops down to help us sift through the ashes to discover treasures, treasures we can take with us as we begin anew.

Without Paul's daring claim, we are left with little encouragement for those who suffer tragic human loss. Without the gift of God's help, many would be left with the poor alternatives of bitterness, self-pity or despair.

Does Everything Work for Good?

But the question remains for us: "Can we affirm Paul's claim?" Can we believe it is true for us and will be true for those who suffer far more than we? Can we say with voices of faith that 'in everything God works for good'?

Life in the Rear View Mirror

Most of us have learned that many things that were traumatic at the time later proved to be opportunities for great good:
- A job that we did not get—and a better one that came later
- A romantic relationship that ended and later was seen as a dead-end street
- A time of illness that helped bring a better perspective on life
- A personal failure that brought new compassion and

genuine humility.

All of us could give personal examples of some experience in our past that seemed tragic at the time but later brought blessings to us. Perhaps in some cases those experiences were even worth the pain and suffering for the good they brought.

Hard Times Can Work for Good

Each of us can readily affirm that *some* things have worked for good, even those things that have brought us pain. Perhaps even some of the things that initially brought us the greatest harm have provided the greatest gain. But Paul is even more daring in his assertion. He is not claiming that only *some* things have potential for good but that *all* things have the potential for good. Further, he does not claim that good *may* come out of it but that good *will* come out of it, at least to those who love God. Paul asserts that the key change agent is God. God, in partnership with us, helps resurrect light out of darkness, hope out of despair, good things out of the dregs of human tragedy.

I appreciate the way the New English Bible translates this verse: "In everything, as we know, (God) co-operates for good with those who love God..." Paul has made a very bold claim about life and God's interaction with us. Is Paul trustworthy? Does Paul know what he is talking about? Has Paul had enough bad things happen to him to put his claim to the test?

Paul's Tribulations

Three times I was beaten with rods. Once I received a stoning. Three times I was shipwrecked; for a night and a day I was adrift at sea; on frequent journeys, in danger from rivers, danger from bandits, danger from my own people, danger from Gentiles, danger in the city, danger in the wilderness, danger at sea, danger from false brother and sister; in toil and hardship, through many a sleepless night, hungry and thirsty, often without food, cold and naked. (2 Cor. 11:25-27)

What do you think? If Paul says, "In *all things* God works for good," has his premise been fully tested? Can we believe his claim that even through pain and suffering God can always resurrect good things?

Old Testament Witness

Paul is not the only person in the Bible who believed in the idea of good coming out of tragedy. Joseph of the Old Testament certainly reflects the same notion when he speaks of his trials and tribulations. Joseph, who was betrayed by his brothers, thrown into a pit, sold into slavery, persecuted because of his moral scruples, and forgotten by those he befriended, spoke these words concerning these events: "(When others) intended to do harm to me, God intended it for good." (Gen. 50:20)

God did not throw Joseph into the pit, but God did help Joseph make the best of it. God did not coax Joseph's brothers into acts of betrayal, but God was able to transform their acts of jealousy into an opportunity to fight famine in a time of draught.

I suppose we all could give stories to support Paul's thesis—if not personal ones, then ones of friends, family, or acquaintances—stories that proclaim that God works for good even in tragic circumstances.

Experience Has Taught Us

Have some of us not seen painful divorces that ended with happy second marriages, or personal tragedy that mobilized the love and support of family and friends, or prolonged illness that offered time to sort things out and get priorities in proper order?

Most of us believe that good *may* come out of almost any situation. We have witnessed such surprising results. We know that good is possible, but often we don't know how. So, in the face of tragedy or crisis we may try our best to think positive thoughts, but we often lack trust in Paul's promise.

Every day one or more of us will be confronted with a real test of Paul's daring claim. At that time, we may want to confront Paul, "Tell me, sir, what good can come out of this?"

What possible good could come out of the death of a premature baby? The miscarriage of justice? The betrayal of a marriage partner? What possible good can come from the atrocities of war, the onset of Alzheimer's, or the tragic murder of an innocent bystander?

Circumstances such as these test our faith when they involve us directly and sometimes even when we hear of such tragic accounts. In any case, I would not suggest that we ever tell those who suffer to look for a silver lining. That would sound insensitive or uncaring to the ones who are deeply hurting. The message of hope must be realized from within. Paul is asking us to accept in our minds and hearts the notion that *in* everything that happens to us, no matter how tragic or painful, God will *work with us* to bring about some ultimate good.

We are asked to trust in God even when our vision is blurred, even when we can see only darkness, even when we feel only immense pain. *In the darkest night of our soul, we are asked to believe in the daybreak of God's grace.*

We are asked to believe the unbelievable—that in absolutely everything God works for good!

A Troublesome Verse

But we have one important verse yet to explore. It is the part of this passage that I have never really wanted to acknowledge. It is the part that says, "...for those who love God." I don't like the way that sounds! It sounds at first as though God is willing to work for good only with those who love him. It sounds like favoritism!

But I do not believe that is what this passage means. Scripture tells us that God "sends rain on the just and on the unjust." God has never really played favorites with his people. Ask the Hebrews! If God played favorites with them, then pity God's enemies!

No, the reason things work for good only to those who love God is because some refuse God's help. God cannot help people discover the good in all things if they respond with only bitterness and self-pity. God cannot give a new dawn to one who hides in the shadowy cave of despair.

Paul's daring claim is in part a matter of choice. We either believe that God has the power to work good in the midst of all circumstances or we do not. Sometimes we believe in such providence because we can see the potential good. Sometimes we believe because we have previously experienced such grace. Sometimes we trust in a good outcome because we believe in a loving and powerful God, a God who will not idly stand by while we suffer.

As Christians we have been given evidence enough of God's power to bring good out of evil, hope out of despair, life out of death. Have we not all heard of the cross? Are we not the people of the resurrection? Do we not know stories of people like Viktor Frankl, Helen Keller? Have we not seen green shoots come out of dry stumps, new life from weary friends, fireweed covering burned out forests?

The opportunities to examine our belief in God's providence and grace are endless. Life will test our creed as surely as it tested Paul's. Our suffering is inescapable.

Yet, will our faith mature so that we will always believe in God's power to bring good out of all things? Will we continue to profess that God works in all things for good to those who dare to believe in his power and who seek his grace?

In November of 2003 my immediate family gathered to discuss the memorial service following the death of my first wife, Lynn Tull, who lost a twenty-seven-month battle with brain cancer. I knew immediately how I wanted the service to conclude. The cantata titled 'Melodious Accord' by Alice Parker had been a favorite of mine since my church choir performed it several years earlier. The music had such beauty and emotion. But it was the words of the piece that were the most endearing. The text was based on a hymn written by William Cowper. The words I had once sung were now a part of my inner being. They had been etched on my mind and heart through the ordeal of my wife's debilitating illness.

> God moves in a mysterious way
> His wonders to perform,
> He plants his footsteps in the sea,
> And rides upon the storm.
>
> Deep in unfathomable mines
> Of never-failing skill
> He treasures up his bright designs,
> And works his sovereign will.
>
> Ye fearful saints, fresh courage take;
> The clouds ye so much dread
> Are big with mercy, and shall break
> In blessings on your head.
>
> Judge not the Lord by feeble sense,
> But trust him for his grace;
> Behind a frowning providence

He hides a smiling face.

Blind unbelief is sure to err,
And scan his work in vain;
God is his own interpreter,
And he will make it plain. [8]

I believe Paul was right: "We know that in everything God works for good with those who love him, who are called according to his purpose."

Based on a sermon of the same title from *Why God, Why? Sermons on the Problem of Pain* by Justin Tull

Tit for Tat; not That!

Matthew 5:43-48

You have heard that it was said, "You shall love your neighbor and hate your enemy." But I say to you, love your enemies and pray for those who persecute you, so that you may be children of your Father in heaven; for he makes his sun rise on the evil and on the good, and sends rain on the righteous and on the unrighteous. For if you love those who love you, what reward do you have? Do not even the tax-collectors do the same? And if you greet only your brothers and sisters, what more are you doing than others? Do not even the Gentiles do the same? Be perfect, therefore, as your heavenly Father is perfect.

Matthew 20:1-15

For the kingdom of God is like a landowner who went out early in the morning to hire laborers for his vineyard. After agreeing with the laborers for the usual daily wage, he sent them into his vineyard. When he went out about nine o'clock, he saw others standing idle in the marketplace; and he said to them, 'You also go into the vineyard, and I will pay you whatever is right.' So they went. When he went out again about noon and about three o'clock, he did the same. And about five o'clock, he went out and found others standing around and he said to them, 'Why are you standing here idle all day?' They said to him, 'Because no one has hired us.' He said to them, 'You also go into the vineyard.' When evening came, the owner of the vineyard said to his manager, 'Call the laborers and give them their pay, beginning with the last and then going to the first.' When those hired about five o'clock came, each of them received the usual daily wage. Now when the first came, they thought would receive more; but each of them also received the usual daily wage. And when they received it, they grumbled against the landowner, saying, 'These last worked only one hour, and you have made them equal to us who have borne the burden of the day and the scorching heat.' But he replied to one of them, 'Friend, I am doing you no wrong; did you not agree with me for the usual daily wage? Take what belongs to you and go; I choose to give to this last the same as I give to you. Am I not allowed to do what I choose with what belongs to me? Or are you envious because I am generous.?'

There is a pervasive mantra in America, a very idealistic notion, that if one works hard, uses all his or her resources, then one can expect a certain level of success. It is often called, "following the American dream." This philosophy assumes that life provides a certain level of fairness and that there is a definite correlation between disciplined effort and commensurate results.

What we Expect from Life

Even though life experiences don't always bare out our theory of fairness, many of us continue to insist that life should be that way. By fair we mean that good behavior or good effort will be rewarded and that poor effort or no effort should receive little or no benefit. We insist that life ought to be fair. We should always get our just desserts.

My wife, Janette, does not like whining—not from me and especially not from our grandchildren. If one of them starts whining about this or that, she is likely to sit them down and introduce them to one of her favorite mantras: "Life is not fair." Janette gave that speech to our grandson, Brandon. When later he started to complain and whine, she gave him that grandmother stare. After a pause and a deep sigh, Brandon grudgingly said: "I know, Mimi. Life is not fair." (Best they learn this mantra while they are young.)

THE PLOT OF THE PARABLE

The plot of the parable of the laborers in the vineyard centers on the theme of fairness, or in this case 'unfairness.' The laborers who work all day become incensed when they learn that those who worked for only one hour got the same wage. The all-day laborers grumbled against the landholder, claiming that they have been mistreated. For them, the only way payment could be fair is for everyone to be paid proportionately to the time they worked. With that plan in place, the all-day laborers would get the most pay and the one-hour workers would get the least.

But in this parable as well as most others, the plot of the story is not the message. This parable is not about how to treat employees. It is about the kingdom of God, and kingdom rules are different from earthly rules.

INTENDED AUDIENCE

Every parable has at least one group to convict or persuade. The power of the parable is to get the listener to be drawn into the story only to realize that as they accept the story, they have thereby been either convicted for their wrong or reminded of their blessing. So, who is Jesus trying to confront and what is the situation Jesus is addressing?

Throughout his ministry Jesus is criticized for eating with sinners and teaching about the kingdom. The Pharisees and scribes objected to Jesus having table fellowship with those they deemed unworthy. They wanted Jesus to extend table fellowship to only those who strictly obeyed Jewish laws. To have table fellowship with those who were lax in the law seemed to bestow acceptance and respect to those who did not deserve it.

Jesus uses the story line of the parable to make a case that the all-day workers (scribes and Pharisees) should not resent Jesus' welcoming those who were sinners or who had only begun to be faithful (the one-hour laborers). If Jesus could convince the scribes and Pharisees to accept the logic of the story, then he would have won his case for open table fellowship.

THE LANDOWNER'S REBUTTAL

The landowner's response to the all-day laborers was respectful but firm. He reminded the all-day workers that he had paid them *exactly* what he had promised. He also insisted that he had the right to do as he chose with his own money. And then comes the zinger: "or do you begrudge my generosity?"

THE REAL MESSAGE OF THE PARABLE

As one moves from the plot of the parable to its message directed to the scribes and Pharisees, one discovers Jesus making a case for God welcoming the sinner into the fold. The implication is that God can do what he wants with his gift of salvation just as the landowner can do what he wants with his money. Likewise, God can choose to be lavishly generous in inviting even the 'unworthy' into the kingdom. So why should one be angry or jealous of God's generosity?

Of course, most of us do not welcome the main message of the parable. If we are honest, most of us favor 'exact' justice, where every good is rewarded and every bad action is thwarted. We insist that God be fair with divine exactness, and foolishly think that such a plan will benefit us the most. But the parable presents a very different type of divine justice, one described as 'gracious' rather than 'fair.'

THE INDIGNANT WORKERS

The laborers who worked long hours are the ones who protest the wages. But why should they protest? They had agreed to be paid a day's wage and that is exactly what they got. Why should they expect more?

They expected more because they 'looked over their shoulder,' which is always a risky endeavor. They saw that the one-hour workers got paid a full day's wage for only working an hour, so since they worked much longer, they were confident they would get much more than that. And when they got the same wage, they were furious. They felt cheated. Their 'expectations' had gotten the better of them.

EXPECTATIONS ARE NOT RIGHTS

Early in my ministry I attended a seminar that was relatively uneventful except for one illustration that was shared. The speaker told of a woman going to her front door one morning and a well-dressed man greeted her and said, "Good morning, ma'am. I just want to give you this hundred-dollar bill. Have a nice day!" For the next three days the woman waited, and each day at about the same time the man knocked on her door and each time gave her a crisp new hundred-dollar bill. On the fifth day the woman saw the man coming down the street. She waited at her door, but the doorbell never rang. Becoming impatient she stepped out on the porch and when she did, she saw the same man at the door of her neighbor. She immediately yelled out at the man, "Hey, where's my hundred-dollar bill?" The seminar leader pointed out that sometimes people try to make their *expectations* their *rights*.

THE DAY LABORERS LAMENT

The all-day workers fell into the trap of expecting more pay and when they did not receive it, claimed it was their 'right.' They aggressively protested that they had been treated unfairly even though the landholder had given them exactly what he promised, a full day's wage. They expected and wanted more.

Kate Bowler in her book, *Everything Happens for a Reason, and Other Lies I Have Loved*, speaks of a 'prosperity theology' that pervades American culture.[9] This theology insists that if we do good, strive for the right, God will reward us with blessings—not simply intangible good feelings, but actual physical blessings. This theology insists that God is 'obligated' to reward us when we do the right thing. And if God fails to dispense blessing with exact fairness, then there are clear grounds for disgruntlement or disbelief. The attitude of the all-day worker still lives.

A TIT FOR TAT GOD?

Many today are advocates for exact justice. They insist that good be rewarded and that evil be punished, both in a carefully calculated measure. They despise rewards that are given out in a careless and arbitrary manner.

But the parable of the laborers in the vineyard firmly rejects such divine favoritism. The God of the parable bestows generosity even when not earned. This God is not persuaded by those who cry foul. Does God not have the right to do as God chooses and to bless whomever he chooses?

JESUS' UNDERSTANDING OF GOD

The parable of the laborers in the vineyard is not the only place one can discover an understanding of God that is not ruled by a *quid pro quo* notion of mercy. In Matthew we discover Jesus' own words explaining the seemingly care-free way God bestows mercy: "God makes his sun rise on the evil and on the good, and sends rain on the righteous and the unrighteous." (Matthew 7:45) And like the parable, God offers no apology to the one who feels maligned. Afterall, does not

God have the right to do as he pleases with blessings and mercy? Even as early as the book of Genesis, God makes it plain who is ultimately in charge of salvation.

> I will be gracious to whom I will be gracious and will show mercy to whom I will show mercy. (Exodus 33:18)

NO RIGHT TO COMPLAIN

One could rightly argue that no one is good enough to deserve God's blessings or the gift of salvation. Even so, some will continue to protest that God should not be too generous to those we deem less worthy. We may even try to remind God of all the good we have done, not just in the final hour, but for most of our lives. But when all is said and done, God is God and we are God's creatures. We have no higher court to appeal.

Perhaps exact justice is not our best option. Perhaps we should ask instead for mercy and not worry if 'lesser ones' will receive it as well. Best we just receive the gift of salvation and be grateful. Maybe then we will be able to give to others, generously and lovingly, even to those we deem unworthy. Maybe then we will be more open to 'love our enemies' and to be as 'gracious' as God is. If this is our hope, then Jesus has a marvelous plan.

> But I say to you, love your enemies and pray for those who persecute you, so that you may be children of your Father in heaven; for he makes his sun rise on the evil and on the good, and sends rain on the righteous and on the unrighteous. For if you love those who love you, what reward do you have? (Matthew 5:44-46)

Based on a sermon of the same title from *Why God, Why? Sermons on the Problem of Pain* by Justin Tull.

Who Is God?

Exodus 3:13-14

But Moses said to God, 'If I come to the Israelites and say to them, "The God of your ancestors has sent me to you", and they ask me, "What is his name?" what shall I say to them?' God said to Moses, 'I AM who I AM.' He said further, 'Thus you shall say to the Israelites, "I AM has sent me to you."

Exodus 33:12-23

Moses said to the Lord, "See, you have said to me, 'Bring up this people;' but you have not let me know whom you will send with me. Yet you have said, "I know you by name, and you have also found favor in my sight." Now if I have found favor in your sight, show me your ways, so that I may know you and find favor in your sight. Consider too that this nation is your people.' He said, 'My presence will go with you, and I will give you rest.' And he said to him, 'If your presence will not go, do not carry us up from here. For how shall it be known that I have found favor in your sight, I and your people, unless you go with us? In this way, we shall be distinct, I and your people, from every people on the face of the earth.'

The Lord said to Moses, 'I will do the very thing that you have asked; for you have found favor in my sight, and I know you by name.' Moses said, 'Show me your glory, I pray.' And he said, 'I will make all my goodness pass before you, and will proclaim before you the name, "The Lord"; and I will be gracious to whom I will be gracious and will show mercy on whom I will show mercy. But, he said, 'you cannot see my face; for no one shall see me and live.' And the LORD continued, 'See, there is a place by me where you shall stand on the rock; and while my glory passes by I will put you in a cleft of the rock, and I will cover you with my hand until I have passed by; then I will take away my hand, and you shall see my back; but my face shall not be seen.'

In our search for the true nature of God, we might first ask what is our present understanding of God? Is our theology a conglomeration of our religious upbringing, the tenets of our culture, and our own insights from life experience? How would we describe God to others? A stern judge? Loving Father? Creator of the Universe? Is our God one who tries to catch us doing wrong? Or is God one who knows us by name and seeks to bring us into the fold?

We might also ask ourselves if our understanding of God has changed or if it has been held hostage by its earliest notions? Do we imagine God as an old man with a beard, as a cloud, as energy, as divine truth? And what has most shaped our understanding? Was it the input of Scripture, or the effect of life events, or perhaps the witness of others? Is our understanding of God basically the same as it was five years ago, ten years ago? Or is our understanding evolving as we try to make sense of how God works in our world? Are we presently content with our faith *in* God and our understanding *of* God?

AN OLD TESTAMENT JOURNEY

In Moses' encounter with the burning bush we can discern a most important aspect of God's nature. Moses as he is tending his flock, sees a bush that is burning but is not consumed. As he draws near God speaks to him out of the bush. God calls him to free his people from slavery, but

Moses is resistant. Listen to Moses' plea with God.

> But Moses said to God, 'If I come to the Israelites and say to them, "The God of your ancestors has sent me to you," and they ask me, "What is his name?" what shall I say to them?' God said to Moses, "I AM who I AM." He said further, "Thus you shall say to the Israelites, 'I AM has sent me to you." (Exodus 3:13-14)

According to Hebrew thought, to know the name of a person or deity was to have a certain degree of control over that entity. Moses had just been volunteered by God for a most difficult task—to free the Hebrew people from Egyptian bondage. Moses wanted some added security if he was to rally his people and face the formidable Pharaoh. But God's answer seems evasive, suggesting perhaps that God could not be under Moses' control. Indeed, God uttered words that strongly asserted God's absolute autonomy. "I AM who I AM."

This brings us to our first Old Testament affirmation: *God is more than we can ever know or comprehend.* Our concepts about God have no effect on God's nature. No matter what our understanding of God is, God will be who God choses to be. We cannot confine God into molds of our own making.

The Hebrew Scriptures present a God who can be known while remaining in part a mystery. Throughout the Old Testament, God's face cannot be seen by his creation. In the New Testament this theme of 'mystery' will be repeated. Paul writes, "For now we see in a mirror, dimly, but then we will see him face to face. Now I know only in part; then I will know fully, even as I have been fully known." (1 Corinthians 13:12)

Not all accept the reality of divine mystery. Some continue to speak of God's nature as though we can understand all of God's workings with exact certainty. They insist that *their* understanding of God is the correct one—the *only* correct one. But God's nature will not be determined by who we say God is. God *is* who God *is*.

SALVATION: GOD'S BUSINESS

When we turn to consider God's gift of salvation, our assumptions are even more at risk. In fact, we do not determine whom God blesses and whom God saves. That is God's business. In the 33rd chapter of Exodus, God makes his autonomy in matters of salvation absolute. "I will be gracious to whom I will be gracious and show mercy to whom I will show mercy." (Genesis 33: 19)

The book of Jonah also suggests that 'our list' of those we deem worthy may not be 'God's list.' In the story God saves the people of Nineva much to the surprise and consternation of his servant, Jonah. Once again, God is free to bless even those whom we deem unworthy. God remains the author of salvation. In the matter of salvation, we have no voice.

GOD AS THE HOLY ONE

The Old Testament reveals many aspects of God's nature—his mystery, his authority over salvation. Equally important is the theme that God is *holy*. Webster defines 'holy' as "spiritually perfect or pure, regarded with or deserving deep respect, awe, reverence or adoration."[10] Because of God's *holiness*, God is deserving of wonder and praise. The holiness of God emphasizes God's glory and majesty.

In today's culture the theme of holiness is often dismissed. Many now see God as so utterly approachable that the notion of holiness seems obsolete. For them, God is not 'totally other' or 'holy,' but more like a 'divine buddy,' one who serves as a personal companion for life. Other present-day theologies suggest that God is the power that enables us to be "the best we can be." In this view God becomes our 'personal trainer' and the Creator is reduced to little more than a projection of our best self.

Some within the Christian Church have continued to stress God's holiness. Through traditional hymnody God's holiness is celebrated as worthy of praise. Their lyrics proclaim God's Glory:
- "Holy, Holy, Holy, Lord God Almighty." [11]
- "Immortal, invisible, God only wise, in light inaccessible hid from our eyes. Most blessed most glorious, the ancient of days, almighty, victorious, thy great name we praise."[12]

How glorious is our God? How holy? How awesome? How deserving of praise? Has our notion of God lost all wonder, all mystery, all glory? Do we worship an awesome God or just a *sweet lullaby version* of the Divine?

I would argue that for God to be the one true God, then God must be more than creation, more than human thought, more than dogma or spiritual ecstasy. And if God is more than all of these, so much more, then God is deserving of our devotion, reverence and praise.

The Old Testament witness insists that we never forget God's holiness, God's glory. It shares images of angels and seraphim and fire and smoke. It speaks of never seeing God's face and being able to live. It makes the direct connection between human history and the actions of mighty Yahweh. It makes it clear that God is not like us. God's ways are not our ways.

DIVINE PRESENCE

But the Old Testament does not leave us with a notion of an all-powerful yet distant God. One of the most dominant themes of the Old Testament, in fact, is the promise of *divine presence* – a promise given to the Hebrew people, to Abraham, Isaac, Jacob, Moses, and the prophets. Time after time, God gives his words of comfort and promise: "I will be with you!" In our text from Exodus 33 this offer of presence is seen at first as a distinct gift to the Hebrews.

> And (God) said, "My presence will go with you, and I will give you rest." And (Moses) said to him, "If thy presence will not go with me, do not carry us up from here. For how shall it be known that I have found favor in they sight, I and thy people? Is it not in thy going with us, so that we are distinct, I and thy people, from all other people that are upon the face of the earth?"

Perhaps nowhere in the Bible is the gift of God's presence more beautifully expressed than in the words of the twenty-third Psalm: "The Lord is my Shepherd, I shall not want ... Yea, though I walk through the valley of the shadow of death, I will fear no evil: for thou art with me; thy rod and thy staff they comfort me." (Psalm 23 KJV)

Ultimately God becomes personal to us by the gift of God's presence, a presence that was realized throughout the Old Testament. In verse after verse we find God described not only as 'awesome' and 'mighty' but also as One who walks with us, comforts us, and empowers us. This same God also 'calls' us into 'covenant.' God promises to be *our* God and walk with us. We agree to be *his* people.

WHO IS GOD?

Today we may speak of God as Creator, Judge, Loving Father. We may conceive of him as the source of all goodness or the initiator of all love. We may believe that God is infinite, all-powerful, unchanging, holy.

Each of us has an understanding of God, one shaped by

our biblical heritage, our cultural surroundings, our Christian experience, and our interpretation of the events of our life. However, our understanding of God remains incomplete. God is *not* who we say God is. God IS who he IS!

But even though we can never understand God fully, we are not to jettison our search. We need to know God more fully than we do now. We need to deepen our relationship with the One who has created us and who calls us.

As Christians we understand that the life, teaching, death, and resurrection of Jesus will help us greatly in our ongoing quest to understand God. Indeed, Jesus has come to 'show us the Father.' Jesus has given us clear glimpses of God's mercy and love. He has reminded us that God still cares about justice and righteousness, that God still offers his presence, that God still provides a source of power.

As Christians, our understanding of God is drastically shaped by the Christ Event. But the God we encounter is not a new God. Behind our Christian images and interpretations stands the God of the Old Testament. Our Christian perspective is only a closer look, a different vantage point. And even looking through Jesus we will still not understand absolutely every aspect of God's nature. Through Jesus we can only see God more clearly.

Who is God? *God is who God is!* But even though we can never know God completely, we must continue to seek God and to know God. God is more than pure deity to us: He is OUR God. We are HIS People. The words of Psalm 150 are fitting words for our lips:

> Make a joyful noise to the Lord, all the lands!
> Serve the Lord with gladness!
> Come into his presence with singing!
>
> Know that the Lord is God!

It is he that made us, (and not we ourselves)
We are his people, and the sheep of his pasture.

Enter his gates with thanksgiving,
And his courts with praise!
Give thanks to him, bless his name!

For the Lord is good;
His steadfast love endures forever,
And his faithfulness to all generations. (RSV)

Based on a lecture given by Dr. Justin Tull at First United Methodist Church, Crossett, Arkansas, on October 9, 1994

Who Is Jesus?

Matthew 4:1-10

Then Jesus was led up by the Spirit into the wilderness to be tempted by the devil. He fasted for forty days and forty nights, and afterwards he was famished. The tempter came and said to him, "If you are the Son of God, command these stones to become loaves of bread." But he answered, "It is written, 'One does not live by bread alone, but by every word that comes from the mouth of God.'"

Then the devil took him to the holy city and placed him on the pinnacle of the temple, saying to him, "If you are the Son of God, throw yourself down; for it is written, 'He will command his angels concerning you,' and 'On their hands they will bear you up, so that you will not dash your foot against a stone.'" Jesus said to him, "Again it is written, 'Do not put the Lord your God to the test.'" Again, the devil took him to a very high mountain and showed him all the kingdoms of the world and their splendor; and he said to him, "All these I will give you, if you will fall down and worship me." Jesus said to him, "Away with you, Satan! for it is written, "Worship the Lord your God, and serve only him.'"

Philippians 2:5-11

Have this mind among yourselves, which is yours in Christ Jesus, who, though he was in the form of God, did not count equality with God a thing to be grasped, but emptied himself, taking the form of a servant, being born in the likeness of men. And being found in human form he humbled himself and became obedient unto death, even death on a cross. Therefore God has highly exalted him and bestowed on him the name which is above every name, that at the name of Jesus every knee should bow, in heaven and on earth and under the earth, and every tongue confess that Jesus Christ is Lord, to the glory of God the Father. (RSV)

When Jesus was with the disciples at Caesarea Philippi, he asked them a crucial question: "Who do *you* say that I am?" (Matthew 16:13) It is a question that each Christian must answer. And there are a multitude of titles to choose from: Son of God, Light of the World, Savior, the Word made Flesh, Prophet, Lord, Teacher, Messiah, Comforter.

THE ULTIMATE REVELATION

After a lifetime in the church and decades of ministry, I have my own unique understanding of who Jesus is. If I am asked to offer a title, I would say that Jesus is "The Ultimate Revelation." Why? Because Jesus *reveals* to me who God is and who God calls us to be. Three passages from the gospel of John give biblical grounding to this understanding of Jesus.

> In the beginning was the Word, and the Word was with God, and the Word was God... And the Word became flesh and lived among us, and we have seen his glory, the glory as of a father's only son, full of grace and truth. (John 1:1, 14)

> Jesus said to him, 'I am the way, and the truth, and the life...' (John 14:6)

'If you continue in my word, you are truly my disciples; and you will know the truth and the truth will make you free.' (John 8:31-32)

I offer these passages not as proof texts but only to suggest that Jesus as 'revelation' is compatible with several references to Jesus. Jesus as 'the Word' and as 'Truth' support the notion that Jesus' teaching is central to Jesus' identity. Indeed, as the *ultimate revelation*, Jesus shows us "the way, the truth, and the life." He reveals himself and thereby also reveals God. "Whoever has seen me has seen the Father." (John 14:9)

I view Jesus as the *ultimate or perfect* revelation because he reveals more clearly than any past revelation the nature of God and the purpose of our living. Jesus' life and teaching have *continuity* with God's earlier revelation from Hebrew Scriptures. In addition, Jesus' words and actions bring further clarity to the nature of God and what it means to be 'righteous.' For example, Jesus does not discard the ten commandments but instead summarizes their ultimate goal: *love of God, neighbor and self*. Jesus raises the bar for what determines righteousness by going beyond outward actions and words to include inward thoughts and motives.

I must confess that I have never asked someone, "Do you believe that Jesus is the *ultimate revelation*?" Even so, this title for Jesus informs how I approach the Christian life. With Jesus being the *ultimate revelation*, his life and teaching become central to my faith journey. In fact, I claim Jesus as Savior not solely because Jesus is the Son of God but because Jesus' life and teaching are *life-saving*. For example, Jesus' words and actions have convinced me of the futility of hatred or revenge and the blessedness of forgiveness and compassion. What Jesus has 'revealed' in his life and message give direction to my life and help form the center of my life's values. I can speak of Jesus as *ultimate revelation* in that he has given me the "truth that sets me free."

GOD'S ON-GOING REVELATION

As the *ultimate revelation*, Jesus stands within a *long tradition of revelation*, God revealing himself and his will for his people. The whole biblical tradition is predicated on the idea that our God is a revelatory God, a God who once revealed himself through the law and the prophets and later through his own Son. Jesus, as *ultimate revelation* would both fulfill the prophecy of the past and be the central focus of the writings of the New Testament. Indeed, Jesus' life and teaching would become the norm by which to judge all other revelation.

I continue to believe in the revelation of the Old Testament with its account of God's interaction with the world and God's people. Even so, in accepting Jesus as 'ultimate revelation,' I give priority to his life and teaching ahead of previous revelation. No other event, no other biblical witness is more central to my faith than the person of Jesus Christ.

To believe that Jesus is the ultimate or perfect revelation of God does not limit the ways God can speak to us. Jesus' witness does not negate the revelations of God as told in the Old Testament. As ultimate revelation, however, it does suggest that we are to interpret previous revelations in the light of the life, teaching, death, and resurrection of Jesus.

Jesus as *ultimate revelation* provides continuity and consistency with all of God's revelation even as it offers new insights into the nature of God and the life God calls us to lead. There is a *consistency* between the witness of Jesus and the witness of the Old Testament. There is a *consistency* between Jesus' teaching and the life he chose to lead. There is a *consistency* between the life Jesus lived and the lives of his disciples following Jesus' death and resurrection. Even today among the most devoted of followers, one may discover lives that reflect the teachings that Jesus proclaimed and lived.

Even though there is a consistency with former revelation, Jesus also brought new insights and new understandings. The Old Testament emphasizes God's presence and God's demand for righteousness. Jesus builds on this foundation making certain we also understand that God is actively seeking the lost and the unfaithful. God is like the shepherd seeking out a lost sheep and a father welcoming home a rebellious son.

Jesus reveals a God who does not play favorites but instead "makes the sun rise on the evil and upon the good and sends rain on the righteous and the unrighteous." (Matthew 5:45) According to Jesus' teaching, this God does not prevent the righteous from suffering, nor does God hinder the wicked from receiving blessings. Everyone will experience both blessings and hardships. God does not even play favorites in relation to his own son. God would not intervene to save his Son's life.

JESUS' TEMPTATION

Central to my understanding of Jesus is the account of his temptation in the wilderness. Jesus resisted temptations here that would prove pivotal to the direction and scope of his ministry.

In the first temptation, the devil tempts Jesus by suggesting he turn stones to bread. To do so, Jesus would have to use his powers to meet his own needs. Jesus refused. In fact, throughout his ministry Jesus would use his powers to perform wonders to others, but never to benefit himself.

In the second temptation the devil challenged Jesus to throw himself off a high place and let the angels bear him up. Again, Jesus refused. He would not use his powers for self-glorification. Later, Jesus would ask many of those he healed not to tell anyone of the miracle. He did not want to draw attention to himself and his powers. His healings were not a means towards an end but rather simple acts of compassion.

In the third temptation Jesus was asked to bow down and worship the devil. With that act would come immense worldly power. But just as Jesus refused to act to benefit himself, he refused to show allegiance to anyone but God.

Throughout his ministry, Jesus would resist the temptations of serving self, glorifying self, and worshipping anything other than God. His life stance would always be one of self-giving love and humility. Later, the apostle Paul would speak of Jesus' nature and how he fulfilled his role as Messiah:

> Let the same mind be in you that was in Christ Jesus, who, though he was in the form of God, did not regard equality with God as something to be exploited, but emptied himself, taking the form of a slave, being born in human likeness. And being found in human form, he humbled himself and became obedient to the point of death—even death on a cross. (Philippians 2:5-8)

THE CROSS EVENT

It is in the event of the cross that we discover a culmination of Jesus' life as the *ultimate revelation*. Jesus' ministry began by refusing to turn stones to bread. Now near the end of his life he would once again reject using his power to save himself. At the same time, Jesus would also bear witness to his own teachings. Remember his words?

> For those who want to save their life, will lose it, and those who lose their life for my sake, and for the sake of the gospel, will save it. (Mark 8:35)

On the cross Jesus refuses to *save* himself. He will not

call down legions to grant him political power. He will not use his cunning or miraculous powers to provide a means of escape. Indeed, his prayer in the garden of Gethsemane lifts only his human desire to be spared. Jesus asks, "My Father, if it is possible, let this cup pass from me..." (Matthew 26:39)

Jesus does not ask God to play favorites or to be exempted from human vulnerability. He does not argue that he should be spared because of his moral goodness. Instead of asking to be exalted, Jesus bears the ultimate form of humility. He takes upon himself the hatred of those gathered around him. While on the cross, Jesus lived out the words he taught. Jesus once told his disciples to forgive their enemies. On the cross Jesus would utter words of forgiveness to those who mocked him. On their behalf, Jesus petitioned God: "Father, forgive them for they do not know what they are doing." (Luke 23:34)

With these words, Jesus reflects not only his own goodness, but also the mercy and forgiveness of God. Did not Jesus describe God as one who would welcome the prodigal home? When Jesus prayed for forgiveness to those who crucified him, Jesus was not asking God to go against God's will. Instead, Jesus' prayer to forgive them was a true reflection of the forgiving nature of God.

THE CALL TO FORGIVE

But Jesus' words of forgiveness are more than a revelation about his goodness and the true nature of God. Jesus' call to forgive is a revelation of what we as God's children are also called to do. Forgiveness is not reserved for the sphere of the divine; it is to be the required action of all humankind.

Through his suffering and death, Jesus showed us that to love fully is to be vulnerable, to be open to pain and suffering. Jesus shows us that God does not play favorites.

God does not offer protection for the saints. All of humankind live in the sphere of vulnerability. Others can bring pain to us, even cause our death. But by the grace of God, death need not have the final word.

The Gift of Resurrection

Jesus, through his own suffering, death, and resurrection brought to us a great revelation—the gift of life after death. Humanity may have the power to bring about earthly death. Yet God has the last word. God can resurrect life out of death. God does not prevent the eventuality of death; God offers instead a reality beyond it.

How can one believe in this revelation that there is life after death? We know that Jesus spoke of the reality of the resurrection. We know of Jesus' death on the cross and those whose spirits were disheartened. More importantly, we know the witness of the disciples who proclaimed Jesus' resurrection. Even in our day we know people of faith who face death unafraid, convinced that the God who is with them in this life, will be with them in all eternity.

Who Do You Say that I Am?

Our key question remains for all to answer: "Who do you say that Jesus is?" Some simply say Jesus is the 'Son of God.' Some will say he is a prophet. Others will call him 'Savior.' I say that Jesus is the *ultimate revelation*. By making that statement of faith, I am obligated to reverently consider all the words Jesus ever spoke, all the miracles he performed, his suffering and death, his promise to be with us always. It also means I must be open to other ways God reveals Godself to us—in the Scriptures of the Old Testament, in the life of the church, in the workings of God in my innermost thoughts and feelings, in the practice of prayer. Even so, the revelations I glean from the life, teaching, death and resurrection of Jesus remain primary. Jesus' witness is decisive in the way I understand God, the way I understand my own calling, and the way I interpret all of Scripture.

I am reminded that this Jesus we are asked to follow did not try to be equal with God. He prayed to God, sought God's counsel, unleashed God's power through many acts of compassion. He became human so that he could show us the Father and call us into discipleship. This Jesus was willing to live as we live, being vulnerable to suffering and injustice. Without him we would understand less of God and less about the life we are called to live. Jesus is indeed the *ultimate revelation.*

Paul clearly understood the true nature of the One we call the Christ. He invites us to follow in his footsteps.

> Let the same mind be in you that was in Christ Jesus, who, though he was in the form of God, did not regard equality with God as something to be exploited, but emptied himself, taking the form of a slave, being born in human likeness. And being found in human form, he humbled himself and became obedient to the point of death—even death on a cross. Therefore, God also highly exalted him and gave him the name that is above every name so that at the name of Jesus every knee should bend, in heaven and on earth and under the earth, and every tongue should confess that Jesus Christ is Lord, to the glory of God the Father.

Based on a lecture given by Dr. Justin Tull at First United Methodist Church, Crossett, Arkansas on October 9, 1994

Is Christianity the Only Way?

Acts 10:34

And Peter opened his mouth and said: "Truly I perceive that God shows no partiality, but in every nation anyone who fears him and does what is right is acceptable to him."

John 14:1-7 rsv

"Let not your hearts be troubled; believe in God, believe also in me. In my Father's house are many rooms; if it were not so, would I have told you that I go to prepare a place for you? And when I go and prepare a place for you, I will come again and take you to myself, that where I am you may be also. And you know the way where I am going." Thomas said to him, "Lord, we do not know where you are going; how can we know the way?" Jesus said to him, "I am the way, and the truth, and the life; no one comes to the Father, but by me. If you had known me, you would have known my Father also; henceforth you know him and have seen him."

For much of my adult life I have been intrigued with the issue of whether Christianity claims to be an exclusive religion, asserting either that it is superior to all other religions or, in fact, the only way to salvation. Growing up in a small town in Arkansas, I had little exposure to world religions. In fact, as an active United Methodist youth, my primary religious experience was within the confines of my local Methodist church. Only on rare occasions did I visit other Protestant churches, and only once did I step inside the local

Catholic church--and then not for worship, but for a joint youth meeting. Growing up in this small town I was aware of only one family that did not belong to one of three main groups -- Protestants, Catholics, and the unchurched. That unique family was reportedly the only Jewish family in our town.

Later, as a United Methodist pastor my interest in the issue of inclusive vs. exclusive Christianity intensified, but now I had a responsibility for representing not simply my personal views but those of the biblical faith and of the United Methodist Church. Would I declare that being a Christian is the only way to salvation and to the gift of eternal life? Are people of other faiths damned because they do not accept Jesus of Nazareth as Savior and Son of God? Would I become a proponent of *inclusive* or *exclusive* Christianity?

OTHER RELIGIONS AND GRACE

In more recent years, the dilemma that has long been my personal concern is now unavoidably a world issue. Today anyone living in a town of 50,000 or more is exposed to religious and cultural diversity. Claims of religious superiority are no longer made by only one or two religious groups but by a myriad of radical factions within many of the world's major religions. Indeed, in the Middle East radical religious factions are currently doing far more than passionately debating religious superiority; they are killing each other as the ultimate expression of their exclusive claims. The issue of *exclusive* versus *inclusive* religion now belongs to the larger world sphere with far-reaching social and political consequences.

A PERSONAL BIAS

In my personal struggle with this issue I must begin with my own religious bias. As a Christian, I believe that the Christian faith best represents the nature of the God of all creation. I view Jesus of Nazareth as uniquely revelatory of the nature of God and of God's purpose for creation. The biblical witness has become normative for all my theological reflections. Even so, I do not think that the biblical witness and the revelation of Jesus are the only revelations of God. I accept that there are many religions that reveal to their followers eternal truths about God and life. Indeed, many moral and theological concepts, as well as sacred texts are held in common by several world religions.

I make no attempt to be comprehensive or systematic in my support of my position of *inclusive Christianity*. In sharing my position, I hope that I can give biblical support to those who have found radical exclusivism incompatible with their own views. It is clear to me after my study of the issue that there are countless scriptures that offer support and challenge to both *inclusive* and *exclusive* positions. It is my hope that my reflections will foster a healthy dialogue among Christians and non-Christians alike.

EXTREME INCLUSIVENESS

Though I am obligated both as a Christian and as a clergy to support my position biblically, I must admit that one of the strongest reasons for being drawn to an inclusive position comes not from the Bible but from human interaction. My leaning toward inclusiveness was set in motion by often being offended by proponents of *extreme exclusiveness* – those who insisted that they were saved and the rest of the world, who did not share their beliefs, were damned. From my perspective, some of these exclusivists who claim that Jesus is the only way to salvation have decided for themselves not only who this Jesus is, but also the precise steps necessary to receive such salvation. I suggest, however, that what these exclusivists are proposing is not, in fact, *Jesus* being the way, but *their version of Jesus* being the way.

Ultimately, their key to salvation rests not with Jesus, but with their own unique beliefs. Suchced with an attitude of superiority and condescension making extreme exclusivism most unattractive. Perhaps two servings of this offensive attitude might illustrate my point.

Religious Arrogance

Early in my ministry I wrote the pastor of another Christian denomination informing him that a young couple who had been members of his church had recently joined our church. In his formal reply, the pastor acknowledged that their church did not recognize our denomination, so he would be unable to "transfer" the couple's membership. *"However," he wrote, "I will transfer their names to the rolls of Hell."* I regret that I immediately wadded up the letter in disgust and threw it in the trash. I wish now that I had saved and framed it to remind me of the maliciousness of religious arrogance!

Religious intolerance can also take its aim at other religions, making a claim, not simply of religious superiority, but of sole proprietorship. One of the most arrogant and ill-conceived comments I have ever heard was voiced several years ago by a prominent Dallas minister: *"God does not hear the prayer of a Jew."* Obviously, this minister had forgotten about one extraordinary Jew, one who studied and revered Jewish Scriptures, one who knew enough about prayer to even teach others to pray. *Surely, God heard the prayer of this most revered Jew, Jesus of Nazareth.* And surely God will hear now all those who share the same Scriptures revered by this holy one. Surely God will hear those who daily lift the same ancient Jewish prayer that Jesus prayed. Indeed, what prayers would God ever refuse to hear? Will he not hear the prayer offered by a Buddhist, a Hindu, a Muslim, an agnostic or even the would-be atheist? From my perspective, every person has access to God.

It is time now to look at a few biblical texts, some that support my position of inclusiveness and others that seem to call it into question. I hope that after such discussion it will be obvious that both positions can produce cornerstone passages to support their own view. In the book of Acts, for example, one can find support for both theological positions. Ironically enough, they are spoken by the same person, the apostle Peter.

In Acts 4:12 Peter makes one of the most forceful statements for exclusiveness: *"There is salvation in no one else (but Jesus), for there is no other name under heaven given among mortals by which we must be saved."* But later in the tenth chapter of Acts, Peter seems much more open to other positions: *"I truly understand that God shows no partiality, but in every nation anyone who fears him and does what is right is acceptable to God."* (Acts 10:34)

JESUS' WITNESS TO INCLUSIVENESS

Central to my understanding of Christianity being an *inclusive* religion is that Jesus himself was demonstrably more inclusive than exclusive in his message and ministry. Jesus reached out to those who were excluded by society – the poor, the outcasts, those labeled as sinners. Jesus also ministered to the religious outcasts of his day, namely the Samaritans. But there was one group that Jesus strongly admonished more than any other—the Pharisees. Most certainly, they were the *radical exclusivists* of their day. They thought they had cornered the market on salvation by strict adherence to the law. Their arrogance was compounded because they believed by following the Law, they had rightfully earned a heavenly reward. They held in contempt those who did not practice their legalistic notion of spirituality. Jesus found such religious arrogance both offensive and damning. He ridiculed these exclusivists by saying that the tax collectors and harlots would enter the kingdom of heaven ahead of them. Because of Jesus' condemnation of religious arrogance, every time I hear someone making a strong case for who will "be saved" and who will not, I become wary of their position, if not their motive. I wonder if they are repeating the mistake of their religious ancestors by making judgments concerning salvation that belongs totally to God.

SALVATION: WHO DETERMINES IT?

The biblical witness, in fact, has much to say about salvation belonging to Creator and not creature! In Exodus 33:19 we find these words spoken by God: "I will be gracious to whom I will be gracious and show mercy on whom I will show mercy." Likewise, Jesus, in his parable of the laborers in the vineyard, makes a similar point about God's freedom to give to each as he chooses. The owner of the vineyard argues with his legalistic critics: "Am I not allowed to do what I choose with what belongs to me? Or are you envious because I am generous?" (Matthew 20:15) Central to both texts is the assertion that the determination of who is saved, and who is not, is God's business, never ours. We may have faith in God's grace to save us. But we have no right to determine who is, or is not, deserving of God's grace.

Even so, there is a human role to play in one's salvation. Is that role simply a profession of faith as some today contend? This position is not the dominant one found in the gospels. When Jesus speaks of those who will inherit eternal life, he often stresses doing the will of God, not professing faith in him. In fact, he is indignant of those who profess faith and yet do not show it: "Not everyone who says to me, 'Lord, Lord,' will enter the kingdom of heaven, but only the one who does the will of my Father in heaven." (Matthew 7:21) Notice here there is no mention of 'belief in Jesus' as the means of entering the kingdom. The only prerequisite is doing the will of God.

Inclusive Teaching in New Testament

Likewise, in Mark we find these words of Jesus: "Who are my mother and my brothers? And looking at those who sat around him, he said, 'Here are my mother and my brothers!' Whoever does the will of God is my brother and sister and mother." (Mark 3:33-35) In light of these words, one might ask, "Are there any who would be excluded from doing the will of God? Need they be Christian? Certainly, the faithful Jews of the Old Testament did the will of God. Might others of different religions be capable also?"

Several times in my ministry when I visit the family following a death of a loved one, a family member will voice a concern about the eternal fate of the deceased. Perhaps they were troubled because the deceased was not a professing Christian or did not attend church regularly. They often spoke of the loving character of their family member but were still fearful that he or she might have forfeited eternal life. In the funeral service I frequently use a text from 1 John as a means of addressing their concern: "Beloved, let us love one another, because love is from God; everyone who loves is born of God and knows God." (1 John 4:7)

So, when we love we are 'born of God and know God.' Perhaps that does not guarantee admission into the kingdom, but it is certainly no rejection slip. Whether one is non-churched or a person of a different faith, loving remains central to the gift of salvation.

A Parable of Inclusive Grace

One Scripture above all others has been central to my understanding of inclusiveness. It is a passage that speaks of salvation not as a matter of belief or conversion, but as acts of loving compassion. It is a message that could be embraced by many religions.

> When the Son of Man comes in his glory, and all the angels with him, then he will sit on the throne of his glory. All the nations will be gathered before him, and he will separate people one from another as a shepherd separates the sheep from the goats, and he will put the sheep at his right hand and the goats at the left. Then the king will say to those at his right hand, 'Come, you that are blessed by my Father, inherit the kingdom prepared for you from the foundation of the world; for I was hungry and you gave me food, I was thirsty and you gave me something to drink, I was a stranger and you welcomed me, I was naked and you gave me clothing. I was sick, and you took care of me, I was in prison and you visited me.' Then the righteous will answer him, 'Lord, when was it that we saw you hungry and gave you food, or thirsty and gave you something to drink? And when was it that we saw you a stranger and welcomed you, or naked and gave you clothing? And when was it that we saw you sick or in prison and visited you?' And the king will answer them, 'Truly I tell you, just as you did it to one of the least of these who are members of my family, you did it to me.' Then he will say to those at his left hand, 'You that are accursed, depart from me into the eternal fire prepared for the devil and his angels; for I was thirsty and you gave me nothing to drink, I was a stranger and you did not welcome me, naked and you did not give me clothing, sick and in prison and you did not visit me.' Then they also will answer, 'Lord, when was it that we saw you hungry or thirsty or a stranger or naked or sick or in prison, and did not take care of you?' Then he will answer them, 'Truly I tell you, just

as you did not do it to one of the least of these, you did not do it to me.' And these will go away into eternal punishment, but the righteous into eternal life. (Matthew 25:31-46)

I would not suggest that entry into heaven is guaranteed by simple acts of charity. Jesus is not talking here about token acts of goodwill, but selfless acts of compassion. The parable suggests that heaven is not for those who profess, but for those who show compassion—those who minister to the vulnerable! In this passage, goodness is stressed and not a formula of belief. Jesus is identifying those who will inherit the kingdom. Ironically, in the parable, those given the gift of salvation are completely surprised. Their motive in ministering to others was never self-serving. The gift of salvation was experienced as a surprising and gracious gift!

CRADDOCK'S LIFE EXPERIENCE

Several years ago, I was privileged to hear again one of the great preachers of our time, Dr. Fred Craddock. In his lecture he told of an experience of being in Amman, Jordan, following an outbreak of violence in Lebanon. He had been re-routed to Amman and did not arrive at his hotel room until 2:00 a.m. He was exhausted. A woman knocked on his door.

"Can we have your room tonight?" she asked.
"Who are we?" Craddock responded.
"We have women and children who are refugees from fighting in Lebanon in Beirut. We need a place for them tonight. Would you give us your room?"
"I just got here and I'm dead tired."
The woman repeated her plea: "Would you give them your room?"
"I don't want to, but I will," said Craddock. And he gave them his room.
He was put up in a little shed out back. The next morning the

woman came with a cup of tea and what she called biscuits. Craddock thanked her for her kindness.

"I want to ask you a question, sir. You said last night you didn't want to give up your room, but you did it anyway, why?"

"Well, being a Christian, you don't just do what you want to; you sometimes do what is right even though you don't feel like it."

And she said, "That's interesting."

Craddock then turned and asked her, "Are these people relatives of yours, these refugees?"

"Oh, no. I don't even know them."

"Then why are you trying to take care of them?"

The woman turned back to Dr. Craddock.

"Being a Muslim, sometimes you don't do what you want to but what you know is right." [13]

For the exclusivist, the parable of the Last Judgment offers a challenge to their position. For the inclusivist, a significant challenge comes from some of the most familiar words in the entire New Testament. The opponents to my position of 'inclusive' Christianity are sure to remind me of Jesus' words from John 14. It is the banner verse for Christians who insist that "It's either Jesus, or nothing." After all, they insist, these are Jesus' own words. Indeed, the passage does seem to be making a strong case for Jesus being the only way to salvation.

> "I am the way and the truth and the life; no one comes to the Father, except through me." (John 14:6b)

No One Comes to the Father...

First, let me affirm that this passage is at the heart of the Christian faith. If Jesus is not the way, the truth and the life, then why follow him? If Jesus does not reveal who God is and how one is supposed to live, then how can he be Savior?

As a Christian, I fervently believe that Jesus is the way, the truth and the life. I can profess that he is the way because through his words and actions Jesus has revealed to me what I believe to be the truth about God and the true purposes for God's creation. But even though I believe Jesus to be the way, I cannot turn to non-Christians and say, "Because Jesus is not the way for you, you are not welcome in God's kingdom." I cannot say to them, "Because you do not recognize Jesus as God's Son, you will be unable to do God's will and unable to inherit the kingdom of heaven." I cannot tell them, "Because you do not profess Jesus as Lord you are bound for hell." I cannot speak such words to those of other faiths. To do so would be both arrogant and presumptuous.

But some would insist that I must exclude them. They quickly remind me that Jesus said, "No one comes to the Father except through me." Yet even accepting this biblical passage as being true, I do not have to jettison my position of inclusiveness. I am most willing to accept Jesus as the 'gatekeeper of heaven.' I am most willing to let Jesus determine who will enter the kingdom and who will be denied. Surely, Jesus knows the difference between sheep and goats.

CRITERIA FOR ENTRY

But what makes anyone think Jesus will only welcome those who call him 'Lord'? How can they assume that Jesus will reject people of other religions if they do not acknowledge him as Savior? Did not Jesus say that whoever did 'the will of his Father' was the same as his 'mother, sister and brother'? How then could Jesus ban from heaven those who are members of his own family?

How could Jesus ban from heaven the very ones who have offered cups of water to the thirsty, clothes to the naked, and given a welcome word to the weary and outcast? How could Jesus deny such compassionate people entry into the kingdom—simply because they have failed to worship him, worshiping instead his Father in heaven? Did not Jesus say that those who show compassion will be the 'blessed ones' of his Father, the ones who would inherit the eternal kingdom?

And what of those who insist they have every right to enter God's eternal kingdom—those who readily remind us that they have professed Jesus as 'Lord and Savior'? Surely nothing more could be required of them! Will Jesus allow all of them to enter, or will he say to those who have failed to live out his words: "Not everyone who says to me, 'Lord, Lord,' will enter the kingdom of heaven, but only the one who does the will of my father in heaven." (Matthew 7:21)

JESUS AS THE WAY

I truly believe that Jesus is 'the way, the truth, and the life.' I applaud the idea that Jesus stands at the gates of heaven ready to welcome those God has deemed worthy and to send away those who have failed to live out God's truth. I know one thing for certain: I will not determine who will be welcomed and who will be sent away. In fact, anyone who feels capable of such discernment should be reminded of Jesus' words -- words not only of promise but also of warning.

> 'Truly I tell you, just as you did not do it to one of the least of these, you did not do it to me. And these will go away into eternal punishment, but the righteous into eternal life." (Matthew 25:45-46)

If this Christian ever makes it to the place of light and comes into the presence of the risen Christ, I hope I will have more to say than, "I believed in you, Jesus." I hope I will be able to say that I have been busy trying to live what Christ taught. I trust my life will have included some 'doing' to go along with my 'believing.' Even so, I am convinced that it will only be by the grace of God if I am invited into God's blessed kingdom. The gift of eternal life, you see, is more about *God-ness* than *goodness*.

And if by the grace of God, I make it to the Heavenly City, whom might I find there? I certainly expect to see Christians and those of the Jewish faith. I expect there will be people of compassion and faith from countless religions – Hindus, Muslims, Buddhists and others whose religions I don't even know. I might even see two familiar faces, a young couple I once welcomed into church membership, the same ones that their former minster had relegated to the *'rolls of hell.'* After all, God's grace is amazing.

THE CRUCIAL QUESTION

That brings me back to my first question: "Does God welcome into his kingdom those of many faiths or only one?"

Such a question is ours to vigorously debate, but ultimately, God alone will decide.

NOTES

1. Gerhard von Rad, *Genesis* (Philadelphia: The Westminster Press, 1961), p. 279.
2. Walter Brueggemann, *Genesis in Interpretation: A Bible Study for Teaching and Preaching,* ed. Patrick D. Miller (Atlanta: John Knox Press, 1982), p. 266.
3. Irving Berlin, *God Bless America,* 1938.
4. Ibid.
5. William Sloan Coffin, *Eulogy for Alexander Coffin,* Public Affairs Television.
6. Ibid.
7. William Sloan Coffin, *Credo* (Louisville Kentucky: Westminster John Knox Press, 2004), p. 10.
8. William Cowper, "God Moves in a Mysterious Way," *The Book of Hymns* (Nashville: The United Methodist Publishing House, 1964, 1966), no. 215.
9. Kate Bowler, *Everything Happens for a Reason and Other Lies I've Loved* (New York: Random House, 2018) xi.
10. *Webster's New World College Dictionary,* (Cleveland: Wiley Publishing, Inc., 2005), p. 681.
11. Reginald Heber, *Holy, Holy, Holy! Lord God Almighty,* The United Methodist Hymnal (Nashville: The United Methodist Publishing House, 1989), no. 64.
12. Martin Rinkart, *Immortal, Invisible, God Only Wise* (Nashville: The United Methodist Publishing House, 1989), no. 103
13. Fred Craddock, Lecture at Northway Christian Church, Dallas, Texas, April 6, 2006.

PART TWO

STUDY GUIDE

INTRODUCTION

The purpose of this section of *Reflections on God* is to offer a tool for group discussion. Though individual readers can certainly use this study guide on their own, it works much more effectively with group sharing.

There are several ways these eight leader/participant guides can be used. One model would be to share them one at a time for eight sessions. The session could be covered in a thirty-minute time frame. The model I will be using in my local church is to have four evening sessions lasting an hour and a half (with short break) and covering two sermons each evening. (I find that people commit more easily to four weeks than to eight.) I also think the longer sessions where I alternate between small group discussion (2-3 persons) and larger group sharing (10 or more) works well and facilitates the group dynamic of honest sharing.

As you will discover in the pages that follow, each session has a Scripture reference which is one or two verses taken from the larger text. I have also offered a theme for each session that captures my main assertion. This is followed by questions connecting with the Scripture, quotes, ideas from the book, application to daily life, and suggestions for further reading.

It is my hope that this book, *Reflections on God,* along with two others I have planned for the series (*Reflections on Daily Living* and *Reflections on the Christian Faith*), will be a good resource for individual faith formation.

Staircase of Heaven!

Scripture: *Surely the Lord was in this place—and I did not know it.* (Genesis 28:16)

Theme: *We are not searching for God as much as God is searching for us.*

Connecting with the Scripture
- Have you ever realized in retrospect that God was with you even though at the time you did not recognize God's presence? Can you share that experience?
- Have you felt God's presence in a time of need?

Connecting with the Book
- Do you agree with the author's theme? Why or why not?
- Has there been a time in your life where you earnestly searched for God? Did you experience God?

Connecting with Daily Life
- In what ways have you encountered God during this past year?
- Has the experience of nature ever brought you closer to God?
- Are there ways you can be more open to God's presence in your daily life?

For Further Reflection
- *Prayer: Finding the Heart's Home,* by Richard Foster

God of All the Nations

Scripture: *And in you all the families of the earth will be blessed.* (Genesis 12:3)

Theme: *God is not only the God of all Creation; God is the God of all nations.*

Connecting with the Scripture

- Do you believe that God is the God of all the nations? If so, does God relate to our nation differently than to other nations?
- How do you respond to Peter's argument that anyone who fears God and does what is right is acceptable to (God)?
- Do you accept Jesus' notion that those who feed the hungry and visit the sick are the ones God will welcome into God's kingdom?

Connecting with the Book

- In reading the author's Credo, what do you find helpful?
- Where to you disagree?
- How has God blessed America?

Connecting with Daily Life

- What are some of the ways you have felt blessed?
- How have you been a blessing to others?
- How do you intend to be a blessing in the coming week?

For Further Reflection

- *Credo* William Sloan Coffin

Why God, Why?

Scripture: *Blessed be the God and Father of our Lord Jesus Christ, the Father of mercies and the God of all comfort, who comforts us in all our affliction, so that we may be able to comfort those who are in any affliction, with the comfort with which we ourselves are comforted by God.* (RSV)

Theme: *God is a God of "minimum protection" and "maximum support."*

CONNECTING WITH THE SCRIPTURE
- Is the text above compatible with your understanding of God?
- Have you ever received comfort from others who have experienced a similar hardship or tragedy?
- Have you ever felt God's presence in times of grief? Could you describe that encounter?

CONNECTING WITH THE BOOK
- When you have faced extreme tragedy, was God's grace sufficient?
- Do you believe in a God of *minimum protection* and *maximum support?* Explain how.

CONNECTING WITH DAILY LIFE
- Have you ever asked, "Why God, why?" when good things happen to you? Why not?
- Can we learn to replace "why God, why?" with "how, God, how?"

FOR FURTHER REFLECTION
- *Why God, Why? Sermons on the Problem of Pain* by Justin Tull

Everything Working for Good?

Scripture: *We know that in everything God works for good with those who love him, who are called according to his purpose.* (Romans 8:28)

Theme: *God does not cause all things, but God works in all things to bring about good.*

Connecting with the Scripture

- Do you believe that what others intended for evil, God intended for good?
- Can you give an example of a situation where God would be unable to resurrect some good?
- Do you believe God sends hardships or tragedies to help us grow stronger?
- Do you believe that everything happens for a reason? Why or why not?

Connecting with the Book

- Do you agree with the theme of this sermon? Why or why not?
- Have you ever experienced the 'daybreak of God's grace in the dark night of your soul'?

Connecting with Daily Life

- Reflect on the trials of your life and determine if you have experienced some good from them.
- Who is experiencing suffering right now that you might help?

For Further Reflection

- *Why? Making Sense of God's Will* by Adam Hamilton

Tit for Tat; not That!

Scripture: *For he makes the sun rise on the evil and on the good and sends rain on the righteous and the unrighteous.* (Matthew 5:45) *Am I not allowed to do what I choose with what belongs to me? Or are you envious because I am generous?* (Matthew 20:15)

Theme: *God does not play favorites. He blesses all and asks that we do the same.*

Connecting with the Scripture
- With whom do you identify in the parable? Landowner? One-hour worker? All-day worker?
- Do you believe that God bestows good things to people who are evil?

Connecting with the Book
- Do you resent the fact that 'bad people' often have good things happen to them?
- Does God reward those who do good? If so, in what way?
- What is the message of the hundred-dollar bill story?
- Have you ever tried to make your *expectations* your *rights*?

Connecting with Daily Life
- Who are the people you resent, dislike, or hate?
- Are you willing to let go of hatred, resentment, or envy?
- What steps will be required of you?

For Further Reflection
- *Everything Happens for a Reason And Other Lies I've Loved* by Kate Bowler

Who Is God?

Scripture: *God says to Moses, "I AM who I AM."* (Exodus 3:14) *I will be gracious to whom I will be gracious and show mercy on whom I will show mercy.* (Exodus 33:19)

Theme: *God is who God is and not who we say he is.*

Connecting with the Scripture
- What does "I AM who I AM" mean to you?
- List at least five words that you associate with God.

Connecting with the Book
- Has your understanding of the nature of God changed in the last ten years. If so, how?
- What characteristic of God is the most descriptive to you? Holy? All-powerful? Ever-present? Forgiving? Divine companion?

Connecting with Daily Life
- Do you experience the 'nudging' of God in your daily life? Have you ever felt God's presence? Ever felt God was urging you to visit a friend or volunteer for a job?
- How can you become more aware of God's presence?
- What role does worship, bible study, service, and prayer provide as you seek to experience God in your daily life?

For Further Reflection
- *God Is No Fool* by Lois Cheney

Who Is Jesus?

Scripture: *Have this mind among yourselves, which is yours in Christ Jesus, who, though he was in the form of God, did not count equality with God a thing to be grasped, but emptied himself, taking the form of a servant, being born in the likeness of men. And being found in human form he humbled himself and became obedient unto death, even death on a cross.* (Philippians 2:5-8)

Theme: *Jesus is the ultimate revelation of God by revealing to us who God is and how we are to live.*

Connecting with the Scripture
- Who do *you* say that Jesus is? What title or descriptions would you use?
- Are the words of Philippians 2:5-11 meaningful to you as you strive to understand the nature of Jesus?
- How is Jesus "the way, the truth, and the life"?

Connecting with the Book
- Is the concept of 'ultimate revelation' a helpful one for your understanding of Jesus? Why or why not?
- What words or titles would you use to speak about Jesus?

Connecting with Daily Life
- Do you have a sense of Jesus' presence in your daily life?
- How would you describe God's presence? As God's Spirit? The Holy Spirit? The Spirit of the risen Christ?

For Further Reflection
- *Thinking Through Our Faith* by David Grant

Is Christianity the Only Way?

Scripture: *And Peter opened his mouth and said: "Truly I perceive that God shows no partiality, but in every nation anyone who fears him and does what is right is acceptable to him."* (Acts 10:34-35) *Jesus said to him, "I am the way, and the truth, and the life; no one comes to the Father, but by me."* (John 14:6)

Theme: *Inclusive Christianity affirms that one who does the will of our heavenly Father inherits the kingdom.*

Connecting with the Scripture
- Do you believe Christianity is the only way to salvation? What biblical passages support your stance?
- In Exodus 33:19 we find these words: "I will be gracious to whom I will be gracious and show mercy to whom I will show mercy." So, who is in charge of salvation?

Connecting with the Book
- The book shares two examples of religious arrogance. Do you agree with either? Why or why not?
- How does Jesus support the idea of *inclusive* Christianity?
- In the story of Fred Craddock's experience with refugees, what causes both persons to do the right thing?

Connecting with Daily Life
- Do you know people who practice other religions?
- Do you believe they can receive the gift of eternal life?

For Further Reflection
- *Making Sense of the Bible* Adam Hamilton
- *Forgive and Forget* by Lewis Smedes

Made in the USA
Columbia, SC
17 January 2019